Y0-BVR-016

'NEW POVERTY' IN THE EUROPEAN COMMUNITY

THE SOCIAL DIMENSION OF THE SINGLE EUROPEAN MARKET
General Editor: Graham Room

The countries of the European Community are building a Single Market which will go beyond economic integration and embody a social dimension also. This, in turn, embraces three key ideas: first, that the fruits of economic progress must be of early and direct benefit to the living and working conditions of the ordinary citizen; second, that there must be specific compensation for the social dislocations which an accelerated pace of economic change will produce; and finally, that in a labour market which will become Community-wide, there must be a concomitant 'Europeanisation' of workers' rights of industrial citizenship.

These developments have been, and will continue to be, the subject of much heated political debate. This series, which brings together some of the important academic contributions to these debates, is likely to become essential reading for social policy academics, students and policy-makers.

John Benington and Maria Grazia Giannichedda
POVERTY AND INEQUALITY: Themes for European Policy
Séamus Ó Cinnéide and Diana Robbins
POVERTY IN THE EUROPEAN COMMUNITY: The National Contexts
Graham Room
'NEW POVERTY' IN THE EUROPEAN COMMUNITY

Commission of the European Communities

‘New Poverty’ in the European Community

derived from a study prepared with the support of the
Commission of the European Communities

Graham Room
Reader in Social Policy
University of Bath

in collaboration with

Jos Berghman
Alfredo Bruto da Costa
Maria Grazia Giannichedda
Helmut Hartmann
Bernd Henningsen
Frank Laczko
Roger Lawson
Luis Vila Lopez
Gregory Mourgelas
Séamus Ó Cinnéide
Diana Robbins
Gaston Schaber
Jean-Paul Tricart

Foreword by
Vasso Papandreou
European Commissioner for Employment, Industrial Relations and Social Affairs

MACMILLAN

First published 1990

Published by
MACMILLAN PRESS LTD
Houndmills, Basingstoke, Hampshire RG21 2XS
and London
Companies and representatives
throughout the world

Filmset by Wearside Tradespools, Fulwell, Sunderland

Printed in Great Britain by WBC Print Ltd., Bridgend,

British Library Cataloguing in Publication Data
Room, Graham
'New poverty' in the European Community. – The social dimension of the single European market.
1. European Community countries. Poverty
I. Title II. Series
305.569094

ISBN 0–333–52295–8

For Pat Collett

Contents

List of Tables

Foreword

Poverty is a major challenge for the social policies of the Member States of the European Community. It is also a challenge to the Community as a whole: the continuing economic crisis has increased and highlighted situations of social exclusion, and the changes expected to come with 1992 require a constant watch to be kept on solidarity and cohesion within the Community.

Since the mid-1970s, growing attention has been paid in the European countries to changes in the patterns and processes of poverty. Various authors, responsible authorities and non-governmental organisations underlined that these countries were faced with new forms of poverty, resulting from increasingly precarious employment, changes in family structures and limitations in social protection.

The creation of the Single Market will contribute to economic growth and, in time, to an improvement in the employment situation and therefore also in the situation of the most underprivileged. By means of its general economic policy, the Community is contributing to this development.

Its effects, however, at least initially, on specific groups and/or areas have to be closely monitored and adequate measures have to be promoted at the appropriate level with a view to prevent increased marginalisation. Through the activities of its Structural Funds the Community can help to prevent these negative effects.

Of course, as this book reveals, the forms taken by poverty during the 1980s vary among different countries of the Community. The problems of the structurally underdeveloped regions differ from those of the regions which are suffering industrial decline and both differ from those of the regions in which the benefits of the Community's growing scientific and technological base are likely to be concentrated. This variation only emphasises, however, the importance of strengthening the social and economic cohesion of the Community's citizens. The social dimension of the internal market is thus a fundamental component of the task which the Community has set itself.

Establishing this social dimension is one of the predominant concerns of the Commission. A number of activities are planned or implemented in this respect. First of all, the charter of fundamental social rights affirms solemnly the willingness of the Community to guarantee a number of rights of workers. The work programme adopted by the Commission to implement it concretises such guarantees at the appropriate level.

Such a concretisation should take place within the context of the principle of subsidiarity. A number of social policies are and will continue to be dealt with at national level. This is the case for social security as well as for policies aiming to fight against social exclusion.

The Community's role in this respect is to promote a greater convergence of social security objectives and policies and to stimulate the debate and develop exchange of experiences and good practices through various programmes.

In the framework of the Council Resolution on social exclusion and the new Community action programme to foster the economic and social integration of the least privileged groups, efforts will be made at Community level to secure more effective political action to protect the Community's weakest citizens. The Commission is working actively to produce proposals likely to be acceptable to all sides and marking concrete progress towards greater convergence between the social policies of the Member States. It is also working on proposals in regard to measures guaranteeing adequate aid and resources for the elderly and for people who are outside the labour market, and to action for social integration of the least privileged groups.

I hope therefore that this book will lead to a wide-ranging public debate in the countries of the Community and I thank Graham Room and his colleagues for their significant contribution to fighting against social exclusion and therefore building Social Europe.

V. PAPANDREOU

Preface

The study from which this book has developed was sponsored by the Commission of the European Communities and was undertaken during the Spring of 1987. The study dealt with the debates about new poverty which are taking place in the countries of the Community; the availability of statistics on the new poor; and the measures taken recently by governments in direct response to the problem of new poverty. For each country of the Community, a consultant provided a report on these topics, within a common framework, and a synthesis report was submitted to the Commission for its internal use.

With the encouragement of the Commission, an enlarged version of this study has now been prepared for publication, in the name of those who contributed to the original study. However, as well as drawing upon the original new poverty reports, it also makes reference to a range of other research materials which have been completed under the auspices of the Commission during 1987–88.

The data which are available for the poorer countries in the south of Europe – Greece, Spain and Portugal – are much more limited than for those of the north. This seriously limits the analysis. More generally, the data which are available for comparative poverty research remain rather limited. The Commission's efforts to develop improved systems for harmonised data collection are therefore of considerable potential importance. Because of these limitations, I am particularly grateful to Demetrios Karantinos for his assistance with the analysis of the situation in Greece.

I am grateful to the officials of the European Commission for making this study possible and for permitting its publication. I am especially grateful to Madame Vasso Papandreou for kindly agreeing to write a foreword. The analysis and conclusions presented here are not, however, the responsibility of the Commission.

Some of the analysis presented here has already appeared in summary form in Room, Lawson and Laczko (1989).

GRAHAM ROOM

Notes on the Collaborators

Jos Berghman is Professor of Social Security Studies in the Faculty of Social Sciences of Tilburg University, Netherlands.

Alfredo Bruto da Costa is Senior Socio-Economic Planning Officer in the Central Planning Department of the Portuguese Government.

Maria Grazia Giannichedda is Professor in the Department of Society, Economy and Institutions of the University of Sassari, Sardinia.

Helmut Hartmann was, at the time of writing, Co-Director of the ISG Sozialforschung und Gesellschaftspolitik, Cologne, Germany.

Bernd Henningsen is Professor of Political Science at the University of Trier, Germany.

Frank Laczko was, at the time of writing, Research Officer in the School of Social Sciences at the University of Bath.

Roger Lawson is Senior Lecturer in Social Administration at the University of Southampton.

Luis Vila Lopez is Assistant Professor in the School of Social Work at the Complutense University of Madrid.

Gregory Mourgelas, Attorney-at-Law in Athens, was, at the time of writing, consultant to the European Commission in relation to its anti-poverty projects concerned with the long-term unemployed.

Séamus Ó Cinnéide is Senior Lecturer in Social Administration at St Patrick's College, Maynooth, Ireland.

Diana Robbins is a Visiting Research Fellow at Bath University. At the time of writing she was a consultant to the European Commission in relation to the evaluation of its anti-poverty projects.

Gaston Schaber is Director of the Centre d'Études de Populations, de Pauvreté et de Politiques Socio-Economiques, Walferdange, Luxembourg.

Jean-Paul Tricart was, at the time of writing, Director of Research at OMINOR, Lille, France.

1 Introduction

1.1 POVERTY AND MODERNISATION

One hundred and fifty years ago, the French political philosopher de Tocqueville surveyed the new forms of poverty which were emerging in the Europe of his time. He compared the then most advanced society, England, with countries such as Portugal and Spain and he came to 'a very extraordinary and apparently inexplicable' conclusion. 'The countries appearing to be the most impoverished are those which in reality account for the fewest indigents', whereas in the richer countries 'one part of the population is obliged to rely on the gifts of the other in order to live' (de Tocqueville, 1835).

De Tocqueville sought to explain this paradox. In the less developed societies, production is for subsistence and is governed by the relatively stable conditions of local demand. In the more advanced societies, in contrast, a growing proportion of the population is involved in industrial production and, as such, is vulnerable to fluctuations in the international economy, which can suddenly throw large portions of it out of work. Indeed, as the pace of economic development accelerates, so also will the vulnerability of these workers increase.

De Tocqueville deduced from this that economic development would tend to multiply the numbers of the poor and to increase the burden on public or private charity. In England, at least, it was clear that since Elizabethan times, public charity had taken the major role in this relief. De Tocqueville gave two warnings: first, public charity on this scale would become an intolerable burden on those at work; and second, it would destroy the incentive to work on the part of the growing body of paupers, creating what would nowadays be called a culture of 'welfare dependency'.

1.2 THE POST-WAR SETTLEMENT AND THE NEW POVERTY

De Tocqueville was concerned with two questions which continue to preoccupy policy-makers a century and a half later. First, he saw that while the new industrial order offered prosperity on an unprecedented scale, for the individual worker the employment on which this depended was highly precarious. Second, he foresaw that popular political pressure might lead the public authorities to undertake large-scale measures of social protection, whose burden on the public purse would grow enormously and which would put in question the incentives of the labour market upon which capitalist development depended.

The welfare states of the mid-twentieth century offered a response to both of these dilemmas. First, governments committed themselves to the maintenance of full employment, in face of the cyclical growth and recession of the capitalist system. Second, large-scale systems of compulsory social insurance were established to provide income maintenance for those outside the labour market: social insurance based on the principle of earned rights, however, rather than charity. As for health and education, these were both removed to a significant extent from the free market and delivered as part of a society's collective investment in its human capital. These rights to share in the work and welfare of society gave a new and richer content to the notion of citizenship (Marshall, 1950).

Coupled with rising material standards of living, these welfare states, based on full employment and social insurance, were widely hailed as a recipe for social harmony and for the dissolution of the class divisions of the past. In the United States in particular, despite its position as a persistent laggard in welfare development, social commentators celebrated the civic reintegration of the working class and the decline of social and political divisions (Kerr et al., 1964; Lipset, 1964). Among European writers there was always a more explicit recognition that these post-war welfare states represented a negotiated truce or settlement among the social classes; and, more specifically, a means of appeasing the working class, with its growing industrial muscle and its political and organisational strength (Goldthorpe, 1984).

Of course, the truce had been negotiated on different terms in the different countries of Western Europe. Depending on these differences, it has come under different sorts of challenge from the recession of recent years. In the United Kingdom and Scandinavia, a powerful liberal bourgeoisie had long sought to ensure that social policy would not impinge upon the ethos of the market place. This tended to facilitate the free development of market relations; class interests and divisions therefore tended to dominate the negotiation of the settlement. However, in countries with a historically less powerful bourgeoisie, or with a powerful Catholic Church, 'the leading concern was to preserve pre-capitalist conceptions of organic social integration' (Esping-Andersen and Korpi, 1984, p. 181). The typical result was the creation of separate welfare programmes for different occupational groups, reinforcing traditional status hierarchies and discouraging class solidarity among wage-earners. Elsewhere again, in countries such as the Netherlands, the settlement between the classes was made against the background of a settlement between the different ethnic and religious groups or 'pillars' which also competed for citizens' loyalties, not least through their control over educational provision and welfare services (Brenton, 1982).

Yet whatever these variations, the truce was always fragile and therefore vulnerable. During the 1970s and 1980s it has come under increasing strain. First, it depended upon the capacity of governments to maintain full employment: not only as the means of guaranteeing security through work to the broad mass of the population but also because in general, social security systems remain geared to the citizen as a worker and to the economic value which the market place puts on him or her. High unemployment has therefore put in question the very foundations of these welfare systems, threatening 'to create two nations: one privileged by work, the other impoverished and disparaged by its absence' (Walker et al., 1984, p. 328). It has forced growing numbers of people to resort to means-tested assistance rather than social insurance benefits: the public charity which de Tocqueville detested. It has also put the financial viability of these social security systems in question, with rising numbers of the population non-contributors.

The truce between the classes depended, second, on the progressive universalisation of social protection and educational opportunity, to cover the entire population: a process which was largely complete by mid-century (Flora and Alber, 1981, pp. 52–7). Yet this failed to assure substantive equality of outcomes between different social classes, even in respect of access to welfare and educational opportunities (Kraus, 1981; George and Lawson, 1980, ch. 8). For as long as economic growth continued, rising absolute levels of living standards and of social benefits might divert attention away from these persisting inequalities; with the deepening recession, however, and with harsher restrictions on social expenditure, they threatened to become more politically visible (cf. Goldthorpe, 1980, pp. 275–6). Demographic trends – in particular, the growth in the numbers of elderly people – cast still greater doubt on governments' capacity to maintain – still less to go on improving – the real levels of social provision.

During the 1970s and 1980s, the terms of the post-war settlement have been contested from different directions. Trade unions and their political allies have contrasted the right to social protection and social welfare with the *lack* of security, rights and powers which the worker enjoys in the world of work and with 'the unprincipled inequalities thrown up by the market' (Goldthorpe, 1978, p. 202). In several countries, for example France and Denmark, social inequality moved to the centre of political debate in the early 1980s, under the influence of their socialist governments. However, the truce has also been challenged from the opposite direction: in at least some countries of Western Europe, governments have attempted to roll back the welfare state, undermining those institutions which had hitherto protected the working class from the naked inequalities and insecurities of the market place (Goldthorpe, 1985). Indeed, with the continuing recession and high unemployment, weakening the power of organised labour, this has become the dominant response, except in such non-Community countries as Sweden (Esping-Andersen and Korpi, 1984).

Within these debates, poverty has returned to the political agenda, as a central point of reference – as in de Tocqueville's era – for judging societies' systems of distributing work and welfare. During the 1980s, social researchers, political leaders and the mass media have pointed to signs that new forms of poverty are developing or that new groups of the population are falling into poverty. According to these claims, high levels of long-term unemployment, economic restructuring and recent social and demographic trends are exposing new weaknesses in the post-war systems of welfare provision and social security; new lines of social division and new patterns of dependency are developing; and financial support for the 'new poor' is imposing an increasing burden on public administration (Balsen et al., 1984; Dupré et al., 1986). The new poor, particularly those affected by the continuing high rates of unemployment, are said to be characterised by their unexpected fall from the protection of the social security systems of which the Europeans are so proud; by the suddenness of their descent from comfort and security into poverty; and by their inability to cope with their misfortune, as witness their debts and their lack of skill in 'using' the systems of public relief (which the 'traditional poor' are supposedly good at exploiting).

For some countries – Germany, for example – the 1980s have seen the first extensive acknowledgement of poverty since the immediate post-war years. In others – for example, the United Kingdom – it is the *scale* of poverty that is new. What is common to these various societies is a fear that the loss of full employment is denying to major sections of the population the opportunity to secure their livelihood through work; and, at the same time, a concern at the consequences for the social fabric of large numbers of people becoming dependent upon public relief. These fears have been much more evident in the 1980s than in the preceding decade, because of persistence of the unemployment crisis.

The benign social stability of the 1950s and 1960s thus appears in retrospect not as the endpoint of industrial development but rather as an unusual calm in the continuing war between the inequalities of class and the rights of citizenship. At the same time, other social divisions have become contested battlegrounds: the relationship between central government and local authority, the relationship between the bureaucratised welfare professional and the citizen, the rights and status of women and of ethnic minorities. How far these latter lines of social cleavage can be explained in terms of class divisions is, of course, hotly debated within the social scientific literature. At the very least, however, these other lines of social conflict increase the complexity of the current 'crisis' of the welfare state and the task of social and political reconstruction that is required.

1.3 THE SINGLE EUROPEAN MARKET AND THE 'NEW' POVERTY

For de Tocqueville, the insecurities of the industrial system arose from the competitive ethos of the capitalist market system, which could, within a short space of time, rob industrial centres of their markets. The recession of the 1970s and 1980s has been accompanied – if not caused – by the shift of economic power away from the North Atlantic basin to that of the Pacific. In response, however, the countries of the European Community are now engaged in an ambitious project to create by 1992 a single 'economic space' – within a more closely integrated political community – aimed at recovering this lost competitivity.

Whether this goal can be achieved remains to be seen. Yet it is clear that the economic restructuring that it will bring within the

European Community itself will be considerable. The Commission of the European Communities, under the presidency of de Tocqueville's compatriot Delors, has warned that at least in the short term, the creation of the single market will bring significant social and economic dislocations, which will have 'very severe negative effects' for certain areas and certain categories of people. It warns of 'social exclusion and marginalisation and the . . . appearance of new forms of poverty' (Commission of the European Communities, 1988b). These effects will, of course, be additional to the already large inequalities existing between and within member states of the Community: inequalities which are such that those countries which are poorest relative to their neighbours tend also to be those with the highest levels of inequality internally.

Faced with this prospect, the Commission has concentrated its efforts upon remedial measures through its structural funds, which support training and infrastructure investment in structurally backward regions and regions in industrial decline. However, it is also seeking to confront the much broader questions concerned with citizenship, social protection and social cohesion which have been central to the debates traced in this chapter.

The Commission wants to guarantee to the citizen of a Community country the right to dispose of his or her labour power untramelled by restrictions of nationality; to take part, through Community-wide systems of collective bargaining, in the decision-making processes by which the workplace is governed; and to enjoy certain basic minimum standards of health and safety in the working environment. These guarantees are all concerned with what can be broadly described as 'industrial citizenship' (Marshall, 1950), raising this from a national to a European level.

However, it is, of course, the relationship between this industrial citizenship and citizenship rights more generally that is of particular interest and that is likely to prove contentious during the next few years of European debate. In particular, what of the citizenship rights – at a European level – of those who are outside the labour market, or in irregular/precarious employment, and whose work situation may, indeed, deteriorate as a result of the economic restructuring that 1992 will bring?

1.5 CONCLUSION

The next two chapters of this book will examine the changing terms of the debate on poverty in the member states of the European Community: exploring, in particular, the sorts of claims made by different political actors that recent trends in poverty are significantly different or 'new'. The middle chapters then summarise the available evidence as to the restructuring of the map of poverty during recent years and the social and economic causes of these changes. The penultimate chapter will examine some of the government responses and consider their adequacy.

However, as this chapter has indicated, much broader questions are raised in relation to social marginalisation and social protection and the meaning of citizenship, in particular in the context of broader European integration. It is to these deeper questions that the final chapter returns.

2 The Principal Discussions and Debates

2.1 POVERTY AS AN ISSUE OF CURRENT DEBATE

For most of the countries of the European Community, poverty is considerably more significant as an issue of public debate than it was in the 1970s. However, the political debate has taken different forms in different countries.

All the original six members of the Community (with the partial exception of southern Italy) experienced a period of unprecedented affluence and economic growth during the quarter century following the war. Full employment and generous social security systems ensured that poverty came to be regarded as a thing of the past. The poverty debate that has developed in recent years testifies to the shock which these countries have felt, as a result of the loss of full employment and the gaps that this has exposed in their social security systems. Poverty is regarded as something new within their recent experience: and as something which, rather than being a mere carry-over from the past, is generated by the process of economic and industrial development itself. In Belgium in 1985, a cabinet minister was for the first time given direct responsibility for anti-poverty measures; and countries such as France and Luxembourg have during 1987–88 launched major new initiatives to deal with this development.

In sharp contrast are countries such as Greece, Spain, Portugal and Ireland, which have long been peripheral to the European economy and have long-standing problems of rural underdevelopment. Most of these countries have had less well developed systems of social security and they are, of course, poor relative to their neighbours. Nevertheless, within their own borders political debate has centred more on questions of social and economic underdevelopment than on 'poverty' as such. A poverty debate has to some extent developed in recent years: for example, in Portugal, involving social researchers, the universities, civil servants in the social ministries, the churches, the trade unions and various non-profit institutions in the social welfare field. However, these political debates are, to some extent, an import from the economically more advanced societies, not least as a result of the programmes initiated in this field by the European Commission itself.

The current debate about poverty is much less of a novelty in one country, the United Kingdom. In contrast to countries such as Germany, Denmark and the Netherlands, social insurance benefits in the UK have during the post-war period been set at a relatively low level. In consequence, a significant proportion of the population has been dependent on social assistance, the nearest thing that exists to an 'official' definition of poverty. This has helped to ensure that poverty has remained an issue in public debate for most of this period.

This simple three-fold division conceals a more complex picture, of course. Italy, for example, is of particular interest because it straddles the developed north and the underdeveloped south of Europe. Sarpellon has pointed to the confidence, in the 1970s, shared with the other founding members of the Community, that economic growth would eliminate poverty and that, indeed, this achievement was already complete; but also to the long-standing preoccupation with the structural underdevelopment of the south. Thus, during the 1960s and 1970s there was a

> widespread conviction that the expansion of production would in and of itself resolve the social problems of unemployment, poverty and backwardness. The only noteworthy debate dating from the 1950s concerned the dualistic nature of the Italian economy. Only later, in the 1960s, did the debate open on consumerism and the model of development. Concerning the problems of income distribution, the debate touched chiefly on two aspects – the wage trend and the North/South gap – while it failed to bring into focus the aspect of the distribution of income by individuals and families (Sarpellon, 1983).

Although poverty has in general become a more significant issue of public debate, it is evident that the language of 'poverty' has been used with caution in many countries. Some of those involved in these debates fear that 'poverty' tends to focus attention upon its victims and to degrade them, rather than upon the circumstances which cause it. For some, 'poverty' tends to distract attention from efforts to deal with wider inequalities in society. For others, again, the moral connotations of the term 'poverty' co-exist uneasily with the requirements of scientific research. Other terms are therefore also being used in some countries, albeit with specific connotations of their own:

for example, 'insecurity of subsistence' (Deleeck et al., 1988). Moreover, much of the debate is concerned with levels of purchasing power and with the various social minimum payments which can help to *prevent* poverty, rather than with poverty itself.

2.2 NEW POVERTY AND THE NEW POOR

In various countries of the Community, particularly but not exclusively the original six members, terms such as 'new poverty' and the 'new poor' became fashionable during the 1980s (Balsen et al., 1984; Dupré et al., 1986). However, it is by no means the same sets of actors who have been involved in these different countries. In Belgium and Ireland, for example, it has been the media, political leaders and particular welfare organisations who have spoken of 'new poverty' and the 'new poor', in order to argue for particular programmes of action, rather than social researchers concerned with serious study. In the Netherlands, the terms are used by researchers and the media more than by government. In Portugal it is the trade unions, the political parties and the Church that focus their attention on 'new poverty', demanding measures to stop unemployment increasing, adequate measures of social protection and higher pensions. In France and Germany, the terms are in more general use, but not on a consistent basis. In Greece, Denmark and the United Kingdom, the terms are used hardly at all. However, even in countries where the term 'new poverty' is not used, it seems to be generally accepted that there is something qualitatively or quantitatively different about the patterns of poverty that have developed over recent years.

The terms 'new poverty' and the 'new poor' have been criticised for diverting attention from the 'traditional poor' or for suggesting that poverty is only a recent phenomenon. Much of the debate is rather vague and incoherent. Nevertheless, it is necessary to start by taking stock of some of the principal elements of 'new poverty' that are cited in these debates, so that these can be confronted with the available evidence. Those involved typically point to five principal elements of the 'new poverty'.

First, they cite the major growth in the numbers of people who depend on social assistance and those living on other forms of minimum benefit. This highlights, in particular, the weaknesses of traditional systems of unemployment insurance in times of high unemployment. Those who have been in employment lose their entitlement to unemployment benefit, usually after just one year; and the young unemployed may have little opportunity to earn any entitlement. This development also raises questions about the *adequacy* of these minimum benefits and the conditions under which they should be paid.

Second, unemployment and insecurity of employment – and hence also poverty – are said to be affecting a much wider section of the population than previously, including those in middle-class occupations. In some countries, indeed, it is claimed that the middle classes as a whole can be seen as the 'new poor', inasmuch as they, as well as the working class, have experienced a loss of purchasing power during the current recession.

Third, these debates cite the increasing numbers of bad debts and rent and fuel arrears. This development is explained as arising in part because many of those who are now living in poverty have never before had to cope on a low income. In addition, as a concomitant of their recent prosperity, they have outstanding long-term credit commitments, notably in respect of house purchase. With a relatively small proportion of their incomes not involved in these long-term commitments, they are obliged to cut back their expenditure first of all in relation to holidays, clothes and shoes. During the 1980s, Dutch debates, in particular, have been centrally concerned with these two closely related themes: on the one hand, the problem of indebtedness; on the other, the purchasing power of the social benefits for which such people are eligible, to meet their basic day-to-day needs (Muffels and de Vries, 1987, pp. 6–7).

Fourth, the increasing number of single parents who are claiming social assistance is cited, as bearing witness to the changes which are taking place in family patterns, but also to their vulnerability at times of high unemployment.

Finally, the increasing number of homeless people – most visibly, those who are living on the streets – is seen as a particularly vivid expression of the new poverty, and one which brings together the new poor and the traditional poor, with their urgent need for immediate relief.

If some of these elements of poverty are new, others are very old. They have evoked – and made fashionable again – policy responses that echo the charitable traditions of old, rather than the citizenship rights of more recent times. Thus, for example, the resorting to food distribution initiatives – in particular, under the auspices of the EC –

has been criticised in several countries as sapping the right to a subsistence minimum, in favour of the appeal to charity. High rates of homelessness have attracted 'traditional' remedies in such countries as France: emergency shelter and soup kitchens. And in the Netherlands, organisations concerned with the homeless have concentrated on providing them with food, temporary accommodation and medical care.

As always, however, public anxiety about poverty does not consist only of charitable concern, but also of fears about the damage that may be caused to the social fabric. In the UK, there is much public concern that many of the disadvantaged – in particular, ethnic minorities – are concentrated into specific urban areas, where they may pose a threat to public order. The recent electoral successes of Monsieur Le Pen in France show how readily ethnic hostilities and fears can develop, when economic difficulties take away from the majority population its sense of security. In some countries, the rise in the number of single parent families has raised fears that the traditional family may be breaking down; and measures to assist such families are sometimes denigrated, as encouraging unmarried motherhood or the concealment of informal unions. The large numbers of the unemployed are portrayed as signs of the work disincentives of the welfare system (Muffels and de Vries, 1987, para. 2.3). These perceptions tend to encourage public policies which have more of a disciplinary orientation.

2.3 CONFUSION AND DISSENSION

Like all political slogans, that of 'new poverty' gives only a superficial coherence to a variety of different social and political preoccupations. Political debate about the 'new poverty' is therefore at times confused and even contradictory. Some of the protagonists have been seeking to reveal the connections between poverty, the systems of social benefits built up during the last half century and the broader social and economic changes that are taking place in the Community. They highlight the way that these changes are exposing gaps in those traditional systems of social benefits and are thrusting hitherto secure sections of the population into the ranks of the poor.

Sometimes, however, the 'new poverty' debate has been preoccupied with the more visible and spectacular manifestations of poverty: for example, the numbers of homeless people living on the streets of our cities. The response has been to launch programmes of emergency relief. Or, again, the debate has often tended to focus upon specific categories of the population, rather than upon unemployment and the changes in family structure which affect many of these different population groups. Here, responses have been sought in terms of changes in the social benefits destined for particular groups of the population. In both cases, the discussion of poverty tends to become detached from contemporary debates about unemployment and the broader changes which are taking place in the labour market and in family structure: and unemployment is viewed mainly as a problem in economic terms and in terms of social stability, rather than in terms of the personal consequences for the unemployed. And in many countries, even efforts to combat unemployment have taken second place to austerity measures to reduce inflation: unemployment and poverty are to be tackled in the long-term only, as a by-product of improved economic performance, even if in the short-term the costs fall heavily upon the less advantaged (Kelleher, 1987, para. 1.2).

Three examples will illustrate these variations. In Italy, during the 1970s the traditional identification of poverty with 'problem families' and individuals came under increasing criticism, against the background of Italy's specific history of industrialisation in the North but continuing rural underdevelopment in the South. Industrialisation and urbanisation were threatening the family as a system of support to its dependent members; and institutions which had traditionally catered for the sick and the deviant were assuming a growing role as a system of support for those expelled from the world of work, but one which confirmed their dependence. Against these developments, the 1970s saw the growth of various social movements seeking to develop modern systems of social protection which would extend and preserve the autonomy and rights of the dependent. Nevertheless, the major political parties and the dominant sections of the trade unions and the Catholic Church have been slow to embrace these views. And indeed, in the 1980s, 'the idea of poverty as an organic, structured, unitary process lost vigour and gave way to the identification of new poverty situations which at the most require specific, partial, rationalising interventions, and the identification of well-defined "risk categories" which, if need be, can be ghettoized' (Brandolini and Razzano, 1987, p. 4).

Denmark provides a second example. Under the social democratic governments of the 1970s, political debate was very much concerned with social inequality and the barriers to greater equality. Particular attention was given to the educational system but also to the broad range of economic and financial mechanisms that are involved in the persistence of low incomes: the distribution of earnings, employment, capital assets and property, the burden of taxes and the effect of public redistributive measures (Abrahamson et al., 1987, p. 2). The 1980s, however, have seen 'a shift in the debate (about living conditions) from the general topic of *inequality* (and the barriers to creating more equality) to a more specific debate about . . . *poverty*' (ibid., p. 2). This shift was in part a reflection of increasing public concern about high rates of unemployment and the consequences for those involved. Yet in much of this debate – at least in the contribution of the Conservative Government – attention has been focused upon the homeless, alcoholics and others who have little contact with the social welfare system; and government has looked to private charitable organisations to take the lead in responding to these needs (ibid., p. 4).

In France, finally, at the beginning of the 1970s, the question of poverty was mainly perceived in terms of poor housing. The existence of shanty towns around the large cities drew attention to a marginalised population which was variously described as the 'fourth world', the sub-proletariat, etc. Such research as was undertaken was mainly linked to the publicity campaigns waged by charitable movements such as Aide à Toute Détresse; or to investigations into sub-standard housing; or to official enquiries into the circumstances of 'problem families'; or to evidence of the 'culture of poverty' (Lenoir, 1974; Stoleru, 1974).

During the period 1976–81, however, before the advent of the Socialist Government, social researchers and civil servants played a central role in developing new thinking about poverty. This work, which was in part associated with the first European Programme to Combat Poverty (1975–80), was centrally concerned with precariousness (*précarité*). This referred to the situation of households which, although in a delicate situation financially, manage nevertheless to avoid having recourse to the social services (Pitrou, 1978). At the same time, some social researchers pointed to the weakening of the social fabric in local communities as a result of the recession, and hence to processes of impoverishment and marginalisation which were developing on a broader scale than could be grasped by the institutions charged with the care of individual poor families. This new thinking rejected the traditional identification of poverty with 'problem families' and the '*bidonvilles*'; and it emphasised the central role to be played by social protection policies and, at the local level, by integrated programmes of social development, to combat the impoverishment of the local community as a whole.

However, if the notion of poverty had been in favour in the 1970s, it became obscured at the beginning of the 1980s. The accession to power of the Left resulted in the adoption of a different vocabulary, embodied in the creation of a Ministry of National Solidarity and a commitment to reducing inequality. In the government report of 1981 (Blum-Giradeau, 1981), there is hardly a mention of poverty: the focus is on social inequalities. Nevertheless, building on the new thinking of the previous period, the government launched integrated programmes of social development of urban areas (DSQ), involving partnership between the education, housing, social work and criminal justice departments, and new initiatives concerned with the social and occupational rehabilitation of young people, aimed at reducing the risks of a dual society.

Only in 1984, as a result of campaigns by the opposition parties and the media, did poverty return to the political agenda; but this time the focus of attention was the homeless and their need for emergency relief. By 1987, therefore, the term 'new poverty' had been displaced and was commonly being applied to traditional – and more visible – forms of poverty. It was, moreover, being used largely by charitable organisations or social agencies which have, for the most part, built their reputations on action taken to deal with traditional poverty: help with food, reception centres in winter, appeals to charity, etc. Whereas, therefore, the notion of new poverty formerly referred to the precarious status of employment and of social protection, by the mid-1980s it was identified increasingly with emergency programmes and it has been used in order to support very traditional approaches to extreme poverty. (See, for example, the report by Wresinski (1987) to the *Conseil Economique et Social* (Economic and Social Council) of the French Government.)

Of course, the priority which was finally given to measures of immediate relief bears witness to the chronic nature of the social distress and the undeniable increase in cases of hardship. But it is also clear that debates which are concerned with emergency campaigns are not simply empirical responses to inescapable realities. Indeed, these emergency measures themselves provoked further questions. The charitable organisations involved stressed increasingly that hostels are at best a short-term response to an urgent need, but not a response to poverty. Local municipalities became increasingly vocal in calling for a guaranteed minimum income, to complement the multiplicity of existing schemes of local assistance. New efforts have also developed to investigate incomes (for example, by the statistical service of the Ministry of Social Affairs, SESI); to assess local experiments in dealing with poverty (CERC, 1988); and to study the stigma attached to social assistance. All of these contributed to the pressure which led the new socialist government, elected in 1988, to give a high priority to the development of a minimum guaranteed income.

2.4 CONCLUSION

As this chapter has revealed, the debates about 'new poverty' are under way in many countries of the Community but they involve a number of different arguments. The absence of a clear statement of what is involved makes these arguments difficult to evaluate. So also, although governments have adopted a number of new measures to deal with poverty, it is difficult to assess how far these address the problem of 'new' poverty, until this is clearly defined.

For the social researcher, one response must be to define more clearly what is meant by poverty and to study to what extent new forms of poverty have indeed been emerging during recent years. This will be the central task of this book, notably in Chapters 4–8. However, if the slogan of 'new poverty' is imprecise, this is in part because it summarises the practical preoccupations of a number of different political actors. In political debate, common slogans – such as 'new poverty' – may serve to express and to mobilise common concerns but behind this common language there lies a variety of shifting moral, material and political interests. The next chapter will, therefore, explore the changing terms of the political debate on poverty in the countries of the European Community, the interests which these debates express and the strategies of intervention which different political actors are promoting. It will examine how the cast of actors and the terms of the debate vary between countries, depending upon a variety of institutional and historical factors.

3 New Poverty and Political Interests

3.1 INTRODUCTION

As seen in Chapter 1, the welfare states of the post-war period represented a negotiated truce or settlement among the social classes, but not only among them. They also represented a settlement between the providers of welfare: public and private, religious and secular, local and national, professional and lay, each concerned to maintain and enhance its role and to consolidate its political and cultural influence. The growth of unemployment and social distress during the 1980s has presented each of the parties to these settlements with both opportunities and dilemmas. And the settlements themselves, always fragile and therefore vulnerable, have in many cases been contested, dissolved or disrupted, even if few clear alternatives yet command general support.

3.2 THE POST-WAR SETTLEMENT: THE CAST OF ACTORS

The post-war settlement was negotiated on different terms in the different countries of Western Europe. In order to understand the debates which are under way in each country of the European Community, it is necessary to know who are the leading actors; what are their perceptions of poverty and inequality; what are their practical, moral and political interests; and, finally, what are the wider strategies of social action and transformation which they are pursuing. It is, moreover, necessary to examine how the internal culture of each of these actors – the self-understanding which the group has forged for itself, in specific historical circumstances – can also limit and constrain the perception of poverty which it holds and the response which it advocates.

For the Scandinavian countries and for the United Kingdom, writers such as Korpi and Goldthorpe have described the post-war settlement as being most obviously a settlement between the *classes*: with the State, through its expanded role in ensuring full employment and in providing social protection, acting as mediator and guarantor of the settlement (Goldthorpe, 1984). The State, through nationalised institutions of social protection, which built upon earlier traditions of working-class solidarity and middle-class charity, secured for the mass of the population some security from the naked inequalities and insecurities of the market place, which had been one of the foremost objectives of the trade union struggle.

Goldthorpe has described how, during the 1980s, the settlement has been contested in Britain from the political right, with efforts to 'liberalise' the social and economic order and to reduce the interventionist role of the State, even if, in consequence, government forsook much of the responsibility which it had previously accepted for combating unemployment and poverty. Meanwhile, however, in at least some of the Scandinavian countries, the settlement continued to be contested from the opposite direction, as had happened through much of the post-war period; with the trade union movement and its political allies seeking to combat the disruptive effects of the international economic crisis with an active labour market policy and with high priority being given to government's responsibility for maintaining full employment (Goldthorpe, 1985; Esping-Andersen and Korpi, 1984).

Elsewhere in Western Europe, however, the cast of actors has been more complex. In particular, the Church and its associated welfare organisations have long been powerful. In Spain, for example, while the role of the Catholic Church and its associated organisations has been declining as far as education and health services are concerned, they remain significant in relation to residential care for the mentally handicapped, aid centres for the homeless, nursing homes for the very old, etc. (Duran and Lopez-Arribas, 1987, pp. 16–17). Other social actors, including political parties and government, have been obliged to reach an accommodation with the Church and its daughter organisations; and nowhere is this more obvious than in relation to the relief of poverty, which has always been central to the social role of the Church and to its 'sphere of influence'.

In countries where the Catholic Church is dominant, especially those whose economic development is only recent, poverty has tended to be seen as an object of *charitable* rather than *political* action. This perception is reinforced by the widespread activity of the Church's many voluntary organisations, mobilising voluntary service by the laity. Thus in Ireland, for example, 'linked to the role of the

Church and its many voluntary organisations in providing services, is the "charity" and "service" approach which characterises social service provision' (Kelleher, 1987, para. 4.1). Poverty – both traditional and 'new' – may, therefore, be extensive, but this does not necessarily mean that it moves to the centre of *political* debate. This also means that the focus in these countries tends to be upon the *poor*, as an object of charity and compassion, calling forth services of an 'assistantial' nature; rather than upon *poverty*, as a feature of social organisation, requiring political intervention aimed at changes in social and economic institutions (da Costa, 1987, pp. 5–6). Writing of Ireland, Kelleher has argued that the 'traditional church ideology [is a] major obstacle to the adoption of a model of service provision which would promote self-help and empowerment' (Kelleher, 1987, p. 18). In particular, it is inimical to the development of an approach in terms of the *rights* of citizenship (ibid., para 4.1).

It is not only in the southern countries and Ireland that the Church plays a major role in relation to social welfare. In Germany, in particular, Catholic social teaching – recognised over the last century, to a greater or lesser extent, within the social legislation of the State, particularly that enacted by the Christian Democrats – expresses the principle of 'subsidiarity'. Under this, the family, the local community and the Church have the first responsibility for undertaking social care. The same principle is respected in the Netherlands, where the Church's teaching has traditionally been accepted, that 'the individual members of the community have their own responsibility to care for each other and only when they cannot fulfil this task should central government take over' (Muffels and de Vries, 1987, p. 3). In the Netherlands, indeed, for much of the present century, several different religious and ideological communities competed successfully with both class and national citizenship, as the principal focus of citizens' loyalties; and at least until recently, these communities were able, through their control of much educational and welfare provision, to maintain the division of Dutch society into several self-contained 'pillars' (Brenton, 1982).

The result is that in areas of the European Community where the Church remains politically and socially influential, social welfare provision (services if not cash benefits) remains to some considerable extent under its control. Thus, for example, in efforts to combat poverty, Government initiatives have played a much larger role in Socialist Wallonia than in Catholic Flanders, and, consequently, so have the local social assistance offices (CPAS) in Wallonia (Vandenbroucke, 1987, p. 71). In Flanders, in contrast, the Catholic Church has developed an extensive network of hospitals, homes for the elderly, welfare organisations, etc. (ibid., p. 72). In Portugal, non-profit making private institutions, very many of religious inspiration, play a significant role in social welfare provision, not least with respect to socially disadvantaged groups of the population. For example, within the network of social welfare services, private non-profit institutions account for more than three quarters of 'places' for children and young people, invalidity and rehabilitation, and old age (da Costa, 1987, p. 21).

It is true that in these various countries, church organisations have been obliged to leave social security – cash benefits – to the state and that in terms of resources, the state sector of social protection is much the larger. It is also true that the financial resources for such services come largely from public sources, even if the Church and its associated organisations can bring additional resources of human volunteers. In Ireland, for example, as Kelleher notes, 'most of these bodies receive some grant aid from the statutory authorities to carry out their work but [they] also have to resort to extensive fundraising from the public' (Kelleher, 1987, p. 14). In Portugal, more than half of public expenditure on social welfare (services in kind, excluding social security) is channelled through these private institutions: another indicator of the scale of their activities, but equally, of their dependence on the public purse. And of the capital expenditure undertaken by these institutions, more than four-fifths comes from public funds (da Costa, 1987, p. 22). Nevertheless, their capacity to appropriate public funds on this scale confirms their power, rather than putting it in question; and their influence on the agenda of public debate, particularly in regards to social welfare, is not in doubt.

There are many other ramifications of this, which cannot be elaborated here. However, it is worth noticing that whereas, in a country such as the United Kingdom, local government developed its powers during recent centuries largely around responsibilities vacated by the Church, notably the relief of poverty and education, in countries where the Church has retained its dominance local government has been slower to develop its powers. However, in countries such as the Netherlands, Italy, Spain and Portugal, recent years have seen efforts to expand the role of local and regional government and in many cases, this has been coupled with efforts to restrict the Church's role in social welfare provision or, at least, to assert the role of the public authorities as a regulatory and coordinating body.

In Italy, for example, until the early 1970s the state and the Catholic Church dominated the provision of welfare services, but there was a clear demarcation between them (Brandolini and Razzano, 1987, p. 20). Among the Catholic groups established after 1969, many were concerned with the political, as distinct from the charitable, dimensions of their work: and hence they were much more interested to develop a dialogue with the public authorities than previously (ibid., p. 30). This development was fostered in part by legislation which effected a radical decentralisation of the state administration in the late 1970s, with local government acquiring increased responsibilities for welfare services. At the same time, this legislation tended to challenge the Church-run private welfare system and its privileges.

During the 1970s and 1980s, moreover, alongside the state and Church sectors of welfare, there has been a very considerable growth in self-managed non-profit-making cooperatives – a long tradition in Italy – which have become involved in welfare activities (Brandolini and Razzano, 1987, pp. 21–6). These organisations have provided a secular model of 'voluntary' or 'self-help' effort which is not identified with the Catholic Church and the philanthropic organisations (ibid., p. 20). 'The debate on the role of voluntary service, which began chiefly in Catholic circles, has ended up by permeating a large part of the sphere of secular culture concerned with the processes of transformation of society' (ibid., p. 20). The development of these secular voluntary organisations has also received a boost from laws that explicitly provide for the participation of voluntary workers in the efforts to achieve the institutional purposes of public services: the law on the National Health Service, and the laws on conscientious objection, the prison system, drug addiction, maternity and abortion. Legislation at a regional level has encouraged the development of voluntary service on a still larger scale. These processes of innovation, with the positive utilisation of voluntary service, are elements of great importance for the debate on poverty.

This section has pointed to the varied casts of actors who have modified the truce negotiated among the major social classes in the middle decades of the present century. In the 1970s and 1980s, however, large-scale social, political and economic changes, including newly emerging manifestations of poverty, have disrupted the settlements reached in that earlier period. Many of the actors involved have faced grave difficulties in making sense of these changes and in responding to their effects, because of the specific cultural assumptions indigenous to the organisation or movement concerned. Within some, there have been efforts to modify their organisational cultures, in order to develop new responses and to prepare for new forms of concerted social and political action. Others, however, have lacked the capacity to respond in ways which go beyond traditional strategies. The remainder of this chapter examines these variations and the role played by some of these actors in the re-awakened poverty debate.

3.3 POLITICAL INTERESTS AND PUBLIC DEBATE

The previous section sketched the varied cast of actors in the different countries of the Community. It is now possible to examine the role that they have played within the recent debates and their moral, material and political interests in relation to poverty.

Political Parties

Political parties have played a significant role in highlighting the issue of 'new poverty', particularly when in opposition. In Germany, it was the Christian Democrats who, in the 1970s, raised poverty as an issue for political debate, arguing that the social legislation of the Social Democrat government had favoured the organised and secure working class at the expense of more vulnerable groups (Geissler, 1976). More recently, with the CDU in government, the trade unions and the SPD have been vocal in pointing to evidence of 'new poverty' (Balsen et al., 1984). In Belgium, similarly, it has been the parliamentary opposition parties, notably the Socialists, that have sponsored the term 'new poverty', in criticism of government restrictions on public expenditure. In France, pressure from the conservative parties helped to bring about emergency programmes of relief for the homeless by the Socialist government during 1984–85.

In the UK, while the political debate about poverty has been long-standing, during the 1980s it has grown fiercer. The opposition parties have regularly attacked the government for the alleged effects of its economic policies and its public expenditure controls – affecting public housing schemes, for example, as well as social security benefits – on the more disadvantaged members of society. Looking ahead, they have offered a number of proposals for reforms in the taxation and social security systems, which are designed to lift people out of poverty and to cater for recent social changes: the increasing numbers of women in paid employment, of single parent families, of disabled and chronically sick people living (and living longer) in the community, of elderly people, of people who have retired before the State Pension age, and of young people spending more years in education and out of the job market.

In its counter-attack, the Conservative government has defended its reforms of the social security system, as enabling help to be targetted more efficiently on those who are most in need. It has also, however, questioned whether it is still meaningful to speak of 'poverty' in modern Britain; and it has challenged the way that the official statistics of 'low income' households have been used in the public debate about poverty. Indeed, during 1988 the political debate about poverty focused upon the changes which the government was making in the statistics which it collects of low income households, with allegations that these revisions, defended on technical grounds, were being made in part in order to paint an over-optimistic picture of the changing living standards of the least affluent members of British society (Child Poverty Action Group, 1988).

Local and Regional Government

Local and regional government have also been active in drawing attention to the 'new poverty', and for good reasons. In many countries of the Community, it is local government that is responsible for the administration of social assistance. It is therefore at this local level that much of the immediate impact of the rising number of claims for social assistance has been felt: local government has therefore had a specific interest in drawing attention to the 'new poor'.

In Germany, for example, the city of Munich faced a 71 per cent rise in social assistance expenditure between 1981 and 1986 (Bolz, 1987, p. 11). Some local authorities are employing unemployed persons in order that the latter can then build up a new claim for unemployment compensation (for which the local authority is not responsible) and so that they no longer need local social assistance (ibid., p. 34). The regional parliaments, as well as the Federal Parliament, have been debating 'new poverty' since early in 1986 and many German cities have undertaken local studies of poverty (Kiel was one of the first, in 1985: Bolz, 1987, p. 11). In Belgium, the requirement on local government to finance half of the cost of the national social assistance schemes – and the entire cost of local social assistance – has encouraged the Federation of Belgian Cities and Municipalities to oppose the reductions in social expenditure sought by the national government and the burden of supporting the poor which weighs heavily on the city budgets (Vandenbroucke, 1987, pp. 20–1). The federation has played a leading role in efforts to bring the issue of poverty to national attention.

The Dutch municipalities are important landlords, many of whose tenants cannot pay their rent, and they own electricity and gas companies, many of whose customers cannot pay their bills. These local authorities, organised in a body called DIVOSA, have jointly pressed for the protection of the purchasing power of social assistance benefits which, although locally administered, are nationally financed. They have also called for increases in family allowances (and even the introduction of family allowances that vary with the income level), information on rent subsidies (15 per cent of the people who have a right to rent subsidies are not aware of it), the reduction of bureaucratic procedures, decreases in gas prices, etc. (DIVOSA, 1984). However, some of their efforts to give direct help – for example, by varying the costs of services according to the capacity of the person to pay, exempting poor people from paying municipal taxes or granting them additional benefits out of municipal resources – have been outlawed by central government (DIVOSA, 1984). And because approximately 10 per cent of social assistance expenditure must be met by the local authorities themselves, 'the growing number of beneficiaries [means that] a growing number of municipalities are complaining that the expenditures for social allowances can hardly be paid and will run the municipality into severe financial debts' (Muffels and de Vries, 1987, p. 29).

In France also, the communes – more particularly, the local social aid bureaux – have been confronted by a rapid growth in requests for assistance. In the early 1980s some of them began to experiment in systems of minimum guaranteed income. In the Autumn of 1984 this reached a head when, faced with hesitation on the part of central government, joint initiatives (the Association of Mayors of the major French towns, churches, charitable associations), supported by the right-wing political opposition at that time, called for an urgent campaign against hardship during the winter of 1984–85. Assisted by media coverage, the debate during the autumn of 1984 laid special stress on poverty resulting from long-term unemployment and inadequacy of unemployment benefit; and it tended to concentrate on the more spectacular forms of hardship. Hence, for example, the importance attached to emergency shelter for the homeless in the government plan which was adopted in 1984 and renewed in 1985. It is also worth noticing that the second European Poverty Programme, when it was launched in December 1984, aroused most attention from the organisations participating in the emergency operations that winter; and that this then coloured the projects which were selected as the French component of the European Programme.

In the UK, finally, social assistance is nationally administered and financed. Local government is therefore not so obviously burdened as on the Continent. Nevertheless, the increasing emphasis on means-tested benefits, together with the rising numbers of people making use of these benefits, has led to the social service departments of local authorities becoming increasingly involved in advising clients on their benefit entitlement and helping them to claim benefits (Walker and Walker, 1987, p. 36). The introduction of a new Social Fund, providing discretionary benefits and loans to low income families, is also drawing the social services departments of local authorities into a more active role in the assessment of financial need (ibid., p. 37). In addition, responsibility for the administration of (means-tested) housing benefit has been transferred from central to local government.

Many urban local authorities have been making poverty an explicit issue for local political debate and are seeking to monitor the whole range of government policies which impinge upon the poor. Some local authorities (particularly those dominated by the Labour Party) have been seeking to develop coherent 'poverty strategies', bringing together traditional local government concerns – the provision of housing, social services, work with action projects funded by central government under the 'Urban Programme' – and research into the growing scale of poverty. These strategies are interesting because of the wide range of policies which are being considered for their potential impact on poverty: not only social service delivery, housing and environmental health, but also local transport, contract compliance (the demand that contractors who supply the local authority should respect equal opportunities legislation and pay a reasonable minimum wage) and the implications of compulsory privatisation of services. These initiatives mean that in the UK, as in the Netherlands, local authorities have been exploring the extent of their powers in the anti-poverty field and have, on occasion, come into conflict with central government.

The practical interest of local and regional government in the new patterns of poverty which have been emerging in the 1980s is not peculiar to the northern countries. Again, however, this interest is intimately bound up with the changing patterns of administrative responsibility which are laid upon these different levels of government; and again, the effort to come to grips with new patterns of poverty has provoked conflicts between central and local government. In Spain, the 1980s have seen major changes in the administrative responsibilities of central and regional government, across a wide range of policy areas. Among other things, responsibility for social assistance and social services has been transferred to regional and local government, some of which have developed programmes to combat the most obvious forms of urban poverty, such as child mendicancy and insecure housing. The budgets are still rather limited, however (Duran and Lopez-Arribas, 1987, p. 12). Nor is this only to be found in respect of urban poverty. In rural areas of Spain, some of the autonomous regions have been exploring the legal limits to their new programmes of land reform, launched in order to tackle the problems of high rural unemployment existing alongside large estates using non-intensive agricultural methods, at a time when out-migration is no longer available as a solution to rural poverty (Duran and Lopez-Arribas, 1987, p. 13).

Trade Unions

In many countries, the trade unions were active in creating the social security system. And in countries such as Ireland, 'the trade union movement has campaigned over the last decade and a half for increases in social welfare . . . It has been a major force getting welfare benefits increased above the level of inflation' (Kelleher, 1987, p. 11). During the 1980s, the trade unions have drawn vigorous attention to the situation of the unemployed, not least because of their fears of declining membership. However, in general they have been principally preoccupied with their own members and with protecting their jobs, their wages and their pensions; and they have found it difficult to decide how far they should campaign on behalf of the unemployed and the poor more generally. Similarly, because the trade unions traditionally concentrated much of their attention on the social security system, centred on social insurance benefits, they have been slow to move beyond this to concern themselves with the non-insured population (Vandenbroucke, 1987, p. 22).

The experience of the Italian trade unions illustrates well some of these dilemmas and limitations. They took part in the general effort of post-war reconstruction; they shared in the euphoria of the years of rapid economic growth; and they ended up sharing the assumption that poverty had been abolished. But while, during the period of growth, they played a very significant part in promoting the expansion of employment opportunities and in creating an efficient system of social security – both of these being central to the prevention of poverty – during more recent years they have had difficulty in moving beyond these two traditional areas of concern. This has been particularly obvious in relation to unemployment, which during the 1980s has been of increasing significance as a cause of poverty.

This failure is because Italian trade union activity is still weighted toward those interests that are more easily represented through the unions' legal and welfare services. The trade unions have, as a result, maintained a strong commitment to protecting employment levels in large plants. Social protection has tended to take the form of special schemes won by different occupational categories, with the level of provision tending to preserve and reinforce the inequalities of the labour market (Brandolini and Razzano, 1987, pp. 9–10). The result is that unemployment hits weaker groups such as women and young people but that few of these receive unemployment compensation (Lawson, 1986).

Only in recent years has the trade union movement pursued a more incisive policy on the issue of unemployment. Some initiatives have also been taken to rehabilitate drug addicts and to ensure that the handicapped, mentally ill and ex-convicts find employment and a place in society. The trade unions have also contributed to the struggle against organised crime and for the economic development of the South. Three of the Italian projects which took part in the Second European Programme to Combat Poverty (1986–89) were run by bodies that have grown out of the trade unions. The three projects, concerned with immigrants (CESIL, Milan), the elderly (CREL, Rome), and the development of marginal rural areas (COOPSIND, Udine), took as one of their central objectives the goal of modifying the trade union movement's culture in regard to these specific problems and to poverty in general. Nevertheless, these initiatives are small in scale and there is as yet little sign of any wider reorientation of the trade union movement towards a concern with poverty.

Only in a few countries, such as Denmark, has this concern been more obvious. There, the trade unions representing unskilled workers were active, during the early and mid-1980s, in drawing attention to poverty among the unemployed and the low paid, stressing the common features of their precarious labour market situation (Abrahamson et al., 1987, pp. 2–3). Unlike many other EC countries, in Denmark the bulk of the unemployed have remained within the trade union and unemployment insurance systems, which are closely linked, and 'have avoided comprehensive existential and political marginalisation' (ibid., p. 10).

The Churches

In those southern countries where the Church retains a socially dominant role, poverty tends to be perceived as an object of *charitable* rather than *political* action. Nevertheless, in Italy, for example, especially following the Second Vatican Council, the focus of much of the Catholic Church's thinking shifted from *charity* to *rights*. At the same time, a loosening of the alliance between the Catholic Church and the Christian Democratic Party permitted the emergence of a much more pluralistic Catholic world, with a wide range of positions in relation to politics and poverty. Catholic grass-roots organisations made an important cultural and practical contribution to these developments. These new perspectives included an appreciation of the structural factors creating poverty and a move away from seeing poverty as primarily an object of Christian charity. To some extent, however, recent years have seen a reversal: with some of the more conservative elements in the Church, supported by the present pontiff, portraying the 'new poor' as a fresh occasion for 'charity'.

In other Catholic countries also, significant – but minority – elements of that Church and its social welfare organisations have been active in these recent debates. This has, for example, been the case in Ireland, Belgium, Spain and Portugal. At a practical level, church-based welfare organisations in these countries have been confronted with some of these new aspects of poverty. In Ireland, for example, the Society of St Vincent de Paul has been prominent in using the term the 'new poor' to refer to the middle-class unemployed; debt counselling for such people has formed a growing part of its practical work. In addition, as part of their traditional concern with the moral well-being of the family, the churches have been expressing their concern about the growing numbers of single parent families, including their particular vulnerability to poverty.

These churches and church-based welfare organisations have been forced to recognise the extent of the need that these clients are suffering. In Ireland, again, among those who in recent years have been receiving cash assistance from the Society of St Vincent de Paul, half spent the cash received on food; and more than 90 per cent spent it on such essentials as food, fuel bills and rent (Kelleher, 1987, p. 19). These organisations have also been forced then to develop new skills in, for example, debt counselling (and food distribution). The Society of St Vincent de Paul has been spending an increasing amount of its time negotiating on behalf of the middle-class unemployed with their creditors, including cases of liquidation and 'trading down' the housing market: skills which traditionally this charity did not have (de Barra, 1984).

In non-Catholic countries also, the churches have expressed increasing concern. The Church of England, for example, has highlighted the evidence of extreme deprivation within many urban areas and has been drawing the theological, moral and practical implications to the attention of its local congregations. Its report, *Faith in the City*, was not well-received by Government; but it is interesting because of the follow-up work it has generated in parishes within congregations, and sometimes between local churches and the local authority (Church of England, 1985).

Private Welfare Organisations

Private welfare organisations, although they may play only a minor role in quantitative terms, play a major part in constructing the public debate. They can also be important for coping with newly emerging problems: after a while, such initiatives, if they survive, 'are taken over by existing organisations [and] the process of subsidising and professionalisation sets in' (Vanderbroucke, 1987, p. 71).

Like local government and the churches, charitable organisations have been confronted with practical manifestations of 'new poverty'. They have been faced with a growing burden of clients, especially among the young. However, it would be wrong to suppose that private and voluntary welfare organisations have all taken broadly similar positions within the recent debates. In Italy, for example, there has during the 1970s and 1980s been a significant growth in secular voluntary organisations concerned with social welfare. These tend, however, to adopt a variety of different approaches to the 'new poor'. Some (together with some of the Catholic welfare organisations which developed after 1969) have tended to interpret poverty, or the social problems of the groups that they deal with (drug addiction, youth deviance, the elderly, the handicapped, etc.), as processes which strike certain groups; and which therefore require an approach which can affect both the conditions of the target group (their clients) and the economic, cultural, institutional and social mechanisms that impinge upon that population group. On this basis, they tend to focus on poverty and the mechanisms which produce it, rather than upon the poor; they have developed services which deal with problems which are common to different categories of the disadvantaged and to broader strata of the population; and they emphasise the importance of changes in social policy and publicly run social services. Nevertheless, there are also many other voluntary organisations – including groups linked to the more conservative elements in the Catholic Church – which tend to focus upon the poor as such; which have been developing specialised services which tend to segregate their clients from broader definitions of need; and which, rather than pointing to the changes needed in public policy instead offer an alternative.

The Poverty Lobby

In most countries there is a variety of organisations representing specific groups of disadvantaged people, including a number of self-help groups. In the Netherlands, for example, there are organisations acting for the disabled, the homeless, etc., which are active in political debate. In Belgium, fears of the increasing concentration of poverty among families with children (see Chapter 7 below) has stimulated the efforts of organisations defending the interests of families, such as the 'League of Large and Growing Families' (BGJG) (Vandenbroucke, 1987, p. 18).

In several countries, moreover, alliances have developed among the various actors mentioned in this chapter specifically to highlight the problem of poverty. It is in the UK that the most well-developed 'poverty lobby' is found, bringing together voluntary organisations, research institutes, trade unions and, increasingly, the churches. Elsewhere, similar developments have, however, begun, for example in both Spain and Portugal. In Belgium, the King Baudouin Foundation has been an important focus for increasing the general awareness of poverty. Its publications on poverty (King Baudouin Foundation, 1987) and its policy proposals have stressed the need for comprehensive and preventive action, oriented to the structural causes of poverty and aiming to avoid stigmatisation and marginalisation (Vandenbroucke, 1987, p. 18). In several countries the movement Aide à Toute Détresse is active, espousing the needs of the 'Fourth World' and bearing witness to the fact that poverty is by no means only a recent phenomenon.

In Ireland too, a coalition has to some extent developed between sections of the Catholic Church, the trade unions and the Labour Party. In 1984, elements of this poverty lobby argued for greater efforts to combat unemployment ('the chief cause of poverty'), reduce inequality and improve social services. In 1986 the first North/South Conference on Poverty (attended by organisations from Northern Ireland and the Republic of Ireland) argued that poor people had been left behind by recent economic development and saw the need for a campaigning anti-poverty organisation to represent the poor (*Irish Times*, 23.7.86). Also in 1986, following the publication of the *Report of the Commission on Social Welfare* (Irish Commission on Social Welfare, 1986) – a comprehensive examination of the whole income maintenance system by a government-appointed body – a National Campaign for Welfare Reform was established to fight for the implementation of the report's proposals. Overall, this lobby has tended to view the creation of a high-spending, high taxing economy as the way forward; but this has hardly been in tune with the dominant spirit of the time.

Nevertheless, it is important to recognise that in most countries it is around issues of unemployment, public expenditure and restrictions on purchasing power, rather than poverty as such, that many of the actors mentioned in this chapter are focusing their energies.

The Media

News is of central importance in setting the public agenda of debate, both in deciding which issues are considered important and in what way those issues are to be reported. For poverty to be considered part of the national concern, the way the media treat it is therefore of vital importance. However, as one Irish commentator notes, 'the poor are frequently either omitted completely from this agenda or presented as an "also ran" category on the inside pages. When they are specifically covered, they may be presented in a highly specific, stigmatized and negative manner' (Kelly, 1984).

The distribution of the free EC food provides an interesting case study of how the press deals with poverty. What was highlighted – in the Irish press for example – was the voluntary nature of the distribution network. No attempt was made to disentangle the various political issues involved, such as the reasons for 'food mountains', why so many people required the food, the small amount of food involved per person, the way people had to queue publicly in many cases and, not least, the State's role in the area of poverty. In this coverage, the only controversial aspect was in deciding between 'worthy and unworthy cases'.

The issue of charity is a crucial feature in the reporting of poverty. It is the appearance of the poor that is emphasised, to the detriment of an analysis of the causes of poverty. For instance, in a series of articles on various aspects of poverty, *The Sunday Tribune*, an Irish newspaper, depicted various categories of poor in 'human interest' stories, devoid of any political or social commentary. As one commentator has noted, by this journalistic convention alone, poverty is 'de-politicized . . . thus re-inforcing the tendency . . . to view the poor primarily in a personal, emotional light, as objects of sympathy and compassion, rather than as subjects for concerted political action' (Gibbons, 1984).

3.4 CONCLUSION

These debates about new poverty are, at the same time, debates about the extent to which the public authorities should intervene in order to relieve need and mitigate the insecurities of a market society. They echo, therefore, the preoccupations of de Tocqueville, with which this book began; and they propose a contemporary re-elaboration of the settlements which were reached in the middle of the present century and on which the social and political order of west European societies were long able to rely.

An analysis of the various moral, material and political interests which have been traced in the preceding pages can reveal what potential there may be for collective action to combat poverty. But of course, it is no less important to take into account the interests and power of those actors who will *resist* efforts to extend public efforts to tackle poverty, and of the means by which this resistance might be diverted or overcome.

This resistance takes two main forms, which are typically although not exclusively associated with employers' organisations and some traditional elements of the Catholic Church. In the Netherlands, for example, employers' organisations have favoured ending the links between wages, legal minimum wages and social security benefits; and lowering the level of minimum wages and social benefits, in the expectation of positive effects on employment. They also advocate greater differentiation in social security with respect to family size: with the existing social minimum reserved for a 'complete' family with two children and the social minimum for one parent families being set lower. These proposals are, of course, consistent with traditional liberal responses to poverty.

It is, however, not only from employers' organisations that resistance to more vigorous public efforts can be expected. The charitable agencies which have traditionally provided relief – many operating under the inspiration of the Catholic Church – have not been uniformly enthusiastic to support an expanded political programme directed at combating poverty. In Italy, for example, among the voluntary organisations which have recently developed on a large scale, there are, as already noted, many – notably those linked to the more conservative elements in the Catholic Church – that prefer to see themselves as an alternative to the State, *competing* with it to provide support to people in hardship. The trend is to favour pacts of mutual 'non-interference' that leave to the voluntary sector the entire moral dimension of efforts to deal with social disadvantage. The poor return to being considered as the objects of private charity; and other members of society are called upon to assist by their charitable contributions. Positive action by the public authorities to tackle the causes of poverty and disadvantage then has only a subsidiary role.

Finally, however, it is important to notice that a new – and increasingly important – participant in these debates has been the institutions of the European Community itself, notably the Commission. The Commission, by its studies and by the poverty statistics which it publishes, has drawn attention to the contrasting performances of different member countries. Equally, by its actions it has highlighted specific aspects of the new poverty. For example, through its scheme to provide free food from its surplus stocks, it has focused attention on poverty as hunger; and by ruling that this food should be distributed through registered charities, it has tended to highlight the role of voluntary effort and the private charitable organisations. The final chapter of this book will re-examine the role of the Community institutions in relation to poverty, taking into account the analysis of poverty which emerges from the next chapters.

4 Concepts, Definitions and Measurement

4.1 INTRODUCTION

De Tocqueville, in his comparative survey of the Europe of the 1830s, was concerned not only with poverty but with the burden that poverty imposed on public and private charity. During the 1970s and 1980s, as the previous chapter demonstrated, those who are today responsible for dispensing public and private charity have been prominent in drawing attention to 'new poverty' in the countries of the Community. The information which they collect in the course of their work, recording the number of calls made on their charity, has served as an important source of material for public debate and social research.

In a number of countries, governments have undertaken broader-ranging surveys and data collection in regards to low income families, but with the enumeration of the calls on public charity always forming a central point of reference. This is the case in the United Kingdom, for example, where until recently the officially published statistics on 'low income families' enumerated those families who were receiving social assistance (Supplementary Benefit – now renamed Income Support – and supplementary housing benefit), and those who, although not receiving such benefits, had incomes below Supplementary Benefit level or only slightly above it (Department of Health and Social Security, 1988b).

The levels of benefit provided through 'public charity' have thus remained central to debates about poverty and 'security of subsistence'. In Denmark, for example, 'the basic pension rate has been viewed as the politically determined subsistence minimum' (Abrahamson et al., 1987, p. 21). In the Netherlands, much of the public debate about new poverty has focused upon the 'real minima', i.e. those households whose total income (wage or social security) is less than, or equal to, the social assistance level. Nevertheless, many governments have been loath to accept that the social assistance level can be taken as an official definition of poverty, because they insist that social assistance benefits are set at levels which are sufficient to remove their recipients from poverty. The United Kingdom government, for example, considers that those who are receiving social assistance have had their needs recognised and met and cannot therefore be regarded as the population of the poor. The German government, similarly, insists that social assistance benefits are sufficient to guarantee the basic necessities of living in modern German society and that it would therefore be quite wrong to equate social assistance recipients with 'the poor'.

Social researchers may criticise the adequacy of the income guaranteed by the state through social assistance, the 'safety-net' of the social protection system. Nevertheless, it is clear that if social assistance levels are equated with an official 'poverty line', an improvement in benefit levels has the perverse effect of making it appear that the population of the poor has grown. (Piachaud, 1988, demonstrates the possibilities – but also the difficulties – of disentangling these real and illusory changes in the population of the poor, in the case of the United Kingdom.) In any case, in many countries social assistance involves a number of different schemes which use different criteria – and different levels of generosity – in defining eligibility. The result is that in Ireland, for example, where social assistance payments can be made under a variety of different schemes, 'there is wide variation in the level of social welfare payments given to families of similar size and composition, depending on the category of payment which they receive' (Kelleher, 1987, p. 18). These variations are 'not linked in any explicit way to the actual needs of the particular claimant' (ibid., p. 18). Where there is a multiplicity of schemes, this can of course also mean that the same people are claiming different benefits, without any method being available for estimating the overall number of people receiving 'public charity', in a way which avoids double-counting. On the other hand, as we shall see in Section 4.8, many of those who are eligible to receive social assistance do not apply for it because of ignorance or fear of stigma. As a result, the official statistics of those receiving social assistance will understate the numbers living at or below that level.

This chapter will be concerned with some of the principal attempts at the scientific study of poverty. These studies may exploit the information collected for the administrative purposes mentioned above; but they aim to provide methods for defining and measuring poverty which go beyond the institutional definitions of public and private charity.

4.2 TRADITIONS OF POVERTY RESEARCH

The definition of poverty – and hence also its measurement – is far from straightforward. The difficulties are in part technical; more fundamentally, however, the use of a definition involves choosing among the various theoretical assumptions about the causes of poverty which underlie competing definitions. Indeed, the definition, the measurement and the explanation of poverty are closely interdependent, as also are the policy implications which the social investigator may draw.

During recent decades, social research into poverty has progressed to differing extents in the various countries of the European Community. In many countries, there was little or no tradition of poverty research until the 1970s. Since then, however, in part in response to the social dislocations associated with the period of high unemployment, a corpus of poverty research has now developed in most countries. This accelerating interest in poverty research has also, to a considerable extent, been a direct result of the European Commission's interest in poverty and of the funds which it has made available for research through its anti-poverty programmes.

Thus, for example, in the Netherlands the main poverty research which was carried out during the 1970s was that sponsored by the EC. The *Sociaal en Cultureel Planbureau* (1980) prepared a national report on poverty, using as poverty lines 40 and 60 per cent of average disposable income (with a series of alternative definitions of the latter). So also, Van Praag (see Section 4.5 below) enjoyed EC sponsorship for his studies using subjective poverty lines (Van Praag et al., 1980). In the 1980s, there has been a dramatic growth in research into indebtedness, homelessness and the purchasing power of low income households. Nevertheless, research at a national level has remained rather scarce (Muffels and de Vries, 1987).

Spain, although with very different social and economic conditions, also illustrates this expansion of poverty research during the 1980s. The first major scientific study was that which was sponsored by Caritas in 1984, *Pobreza y Marginacion* (Poverty and Marginalisation), based upon a nationwide survey (Caritas Española, 1984). Since then, some of the regional authorities have sponsored further research into the poverty in their areas: for example, the Basque country and Catalonia. The entry of Spain into the EC is, of course, only very recent; but the Commission of the European Communities has been devoting additional resources to poverty research in the new member states and, together with Caritas and some of the regional governments, seems likely to promote a considerable expansion in the range of research studies available.

In France, many researchers have long been sceptical as to the value and the feasibility of counting the numbers of the poor. Nevertheless, even here attitudes seem to be changing, with various recent studies aiming to improve statistical information in this field. This development has been prompted on the one hand by the increased visibility of some aspects of poverty – homelessness, for example – and, on the other hand, by the lack of information available to policy-makers for establishing the extent of the need for a minimum guaranteed income, an issue much in public debate during the 1980s.

It is, however, the Anglo-Saxon debate that has been most influential. In the United Kingdom there is a longstanding tradition of social enquiry into poverty, which has focused upon enumeration of the numbers of the population falling below some 'poverty line' defined in money terms. Charles Booth in the 1880s and Seebohm Rowntree have traditionally been seen as the pioneers of this tradition (but see Veit-Wilson, 1986); its most recent major exponent is Peter Townsend, with his study of *Poverty in the United Kingdom* (1979).

It is by reference to this tradition that we can explore some of the main definitional questions which arise in relation to poverty. These questions have in recent years been debated with renewed vigour: the relationship between relative and absolute definitions; the place of subjective and objective measures; the relevance of income as an indicator of poverty (Donnison, 1988; Ringen, 1988; Sen, 1983). Within the scientific community, there seems to be as much dissension as ever. Yet these are questions on which the European institutions which are responsible for data collection will need to take a position, if they are to provide the Community information base on poverty to which they aspire.

4.3 ABSOLUTE AND RELATIVE POVERTY

In the United States, the social security administration and the poverty research community have chosen to rely upon an 'absolute' definition of poverty, established with reference to the expenditure patterns of low-income households in the immediate post-war period and updated only in line with inflation. According to this definition the proportion of the population in poverty fell steadily during the 1960s and 1970s, only to rise in the early 1980s. It is worth noticing that this poverty line appears to have gained much broader acceptance in American public debates than has any counterpart in the countries of the European Community and this is perhaps in part attributable to its 'absolute' character (Ruggles and Marton, 1986; Sawhill, 1988).

Absolute definitions of poverty are also being used in studies within the European Community countries. For example, when Hansen (1986) studied poverty among Danes, he used a rather stringent definition which tended to recognise only physical (especially nutritional) but not social needs. In his sample of 29–79 year olds, 11 per cent fell below his monthly poverty line; and when he also applied a second condition in terms of year-long income, this percentage fell to around 3 per cent. This figure is of course a lot lower than the estimate produced by the Danish Low Income Commission, which found, using a poverty definition of 50 per cent of average disposable income, that even in the late 1970s, approximately 13 per cent of Danes were poor (Abrahamson et al., 1987, p. 2).

The absolutist tradition commonly looks back to Rowntree and Booth as its founders. They attempted to discover the minimum income which an individual, a family or a household would require in order to obtain the physical necessities of life. Rowntree's successive surveys, over half a century, revealed a declining proportion of the population of York living in such 'absolute' poverty. During the post-war period, Townsend has sought to promote a *relative* definition of poverty, which recognises that the needs which an individual or family must satisfy in order to live as a member of his society are socially rather than physically determined. Veit-Wilson has recently demonstrated that, contrary to conventional interpretations of his work, Rowntree was only too aware of the relative elements in the definition of poverty (Veit-Wilson, 1986). Nevertheless, what is distinctive about Townsend's approach is that the criteria for defining poverty, instead of being chosen by social researchers, are derived from surveys of social actors' own perceptions and experience of deprivation.

In contrast to the American tradition, the Council of Ministers of the European Community, when it authorised the second Community programme to combat poverty, provided a definition of 'the poor' which stands, broadly speaking, within the Townsend tradition of 'relative' poverty: '"the poor" shall be taken to mean persons, families and groups of persons whose resources (material, cultural and social) are so limited as to exclude them from the minimum acceptable way of life in the Member State in which they live' (Council of the European Communities, 1984, Article 1.2). Indeed, already in 1981, at the end of the first European Programme, the Commission published estimates of the numbers of poor people in the nine Community countries in the mid-1970s, using for this purpose a set of poverty lines defined as 50 per cent of average disposable income in each of the countries concerned. This exercise was replicated recently and produced a figure of almost 44 million poor people in the Community of twelve countries (see Section 5.2).

These estimates were technically respectable and politically courageous; and it is to be hoped that the Commission will continue, at regular intervals, to provide further estimates of this sort. Nevertheless, it is of course difficult to defend this particular poverty line, 50 per cent of average disposable income, as having any particular significance. Forty or 60 per cent of average disposable income would have just as much – or just as little – claim to consideration, in the absence of any sociological evidence that it is at this level of income that the persons concerned are indeed excluded from 'the minimum acceptable way of life in the Member State in which they live'; and Nolan, for example, has shown that depending on which of these lines is chosen, the estimates of the numbers in poverty – at least in his own country of Ireland – will vary dramatically (Nolan, 1989). Indeed, in its 1981 report, at the end of the first Community programme to combat poverty, the Commission made some use of these alternative poverty lines when examining, for example, the composition of the poor population (Commission of the European Communities, 1981). So also, the Commission's decision to operationalise this definition of poverty on a national basis – rather than for the Community as a whole – involved further choices which could, just as well, have been made differently.

It can also be argued that the thorough-going relativistic definition employed by the Council of Ministers misses certain important but 'absolute' elements in the changing map of poverty. The 1980s have seen three new members added to the European Community: countries where 'absolute' poverty has remained significant in recent times, even if there, too, absolute poverty has been declining as economic development proceeds (Karantinos, 1987). At the same time, in the northern countries the growing problem of homelessness reminds us that many of those who fall below the 'relative' poverty line are in such miserable conditions that they would also fall within even the most stringent of 'absolute' definitions of poverty.

Taking all these points into account, it would seem desirable in future, if the data can be gathered, to have a variety of different indicators, both relative and absolute, in order to monitor the changing incidence of poverty in the Community countries. These might take into account the proportion of individual households' income which is spent on food, as an indicator of absolute poverty (Karantinos, 1987, p. 3); but just as significant, if we heed the recent debates on the distinguishing features of 'new poverty', may be the proportion of individual households' expenditure that is tied up in long-term commitments, unavailable to meet immediate consumption needs in times of hardship (Muffels and de Vries, 1987, p. 6).

4.4 FINANCIAL AND MULTI-DIMENSIONAL POVERTY

There are a number of technical problems with using financial poverty lines of the conventional type. Data on income are often unreliable, partly because they are in general derived from tax returns. In Greece, for example, for a large part of the household population total recorded consumption expenditure exceeds reported income: something that is apparently partly attributable to the unofficial economy. In rural areas, moreover – and of course, with the expansion to the south, this is true of a significant area of the European Community – incomes in kind are often of considerable significance. Information as to the cash incomes which people receive may give a very inaccurate picture of the resources at their disposal.

In addition to these technical problems, however, there are a number of more fundamental and theoretical problems. In a pure system of market exchange – which has never, of course, existed – an individual's life chances depend entirely upon the goods and services which he or she can offer for sale. Poverty and deprivation may involve and may, indeed, be defined in terms of a multitude of deficits – lack of food and shelter, of access to health care and education, etc. – but the poor can be identified empirically by their lack of money or of goods and services which can be converted into money.

How far does this hold also for societies where individuals' life chances do *not* depend solely upon their marketable resources? This question has been at the centre of one of the most furious of recent debates. Townsend has argued that below a certain level of income –

a level significantly higher than the social assistance minimum which is provided in the United Kingdom – an individual's risk of being 'deprived of enjoying the benefits and participating in the activities customary in society' increases dramatically (Townsend, 1979). Against this, Piachaud (1981) and others have argued that no such sudden increase of risk can be empirically identified, still less can it be said to correspond to a particular level of income.

This debate continues. At the very least, it should discourage the social statisticians of the European Community from giving their attention exclusively to financial indicators of deprivation: and it should encourage them to collect data about other aspects of social and economic disadvantage also. For example, in relation to the structurally underdeveloped countries, da Costa argues the relevance to poverty research of data concerning such simple amenities as piped water and a sewage system. 'Not all the dimensions [of poverty] are adequately covered by a poverty line based on income or expenditure' (da Costa, 1986, p. 13).

4.5 OBJECTIVE AND SUBJECTIVE POVERTY

The aforementioned definitions of poverty involve judgements by social researchers – albeit judgements based upon careful empirical study of the ways of life of different sections of the population. Some researchers, however, have sought to investigate the subjective perceptions of poverty held by the social actors themselves: and they have incorporated these judgements into the definitions of poverty used for purposes of research (Room, 1982; Veit-Wilson, 1987). It is claimed that this avoids the imposition of the researcher's own value judgements; and that it allows some 'democratic' decision as to what is to count as poverty. This, in turn, is said to ensure that the resulting account of poverty will be relevant to policy-makers, because it takes account of the subjective perceptions of social actors, whose support for any new policy initiatives will determine how effective those initiatives can be. It can, however, also mean that in times of austerity, there is a downward adjustment of expectations among the population generally: and this can, indeed, produce falling numbers of 'poor', at a time when the lower income groups are in fact suffering increasing hardship (Vandenbroucke, 1987, p. 32).

This aim is carried out in various ways. Mack and Lansley address themselves to a general sample of the UK population, asking them to identify things 'which you think are necessary, and which all adults should be able to afford and which they should not have to do without' (Mack and Lansley, 1985, p. 294). Having established that there is a broad consensus as to this list of necessities, Mack and Lansley then investigate how many people are unwillingly deprived of several of these necessities: who, in the words of the Council of Ministers of the European Community, is 'excluded . . . from the minimum acceptable way of life in the Member State in which they live'.

Van Praag, working in the Netherlands, has been the other most influential point of reference for 'subjective' definitions of poverty. He, too, addresses himself to a general sample of the population, but rather than seeking to identify a list of agreed 'necessities', he asks each person what income he or she would need in order to 'make ends meet'. Van Praag then examines at what level of respondents' income, on average, the income received equates to the minimum income which the respondents say they need to 'make ends meet': this is taken as being the poverty line defined by the *vox populi* (Room, 1982).

Among the activities which are being funded by the Commission of the European Communities, as part of its programme to combat poverty, is a set of studies designed to test out a number of different 'poverty lines', in seven different countries. These studies, coordinated by Professor Deleeck at the University of Antwerp, include a variety of 'objective' and 'subjective' measures (Deleeck et al., 1988). They are likely to provide one of the points of reference for the Commission, as it develops its harmonised systems of data concerned with poverty.

4.6 INDIVIDUAL AND HOUSEHOLD POVERTY

Whatever definition of poverty is chosen, absolute or relative, and however far 'subjective' elements are incorporated, the investigator needs to decide whether to deal with individuals or with households; and what assumptions to make about the pooling of resources within the household. This choice can have important consequences for the poverty trends that the researcher reveals. Nolan (1987, 1989), for example, in tracing the evolution of poverty in Ireland between 1973 and 1980, using a variety of poverty lines (set at 40, 50 and 60 per cent of average disposable income), shows that this period saw a considerable fall in the poverty rate for households, but in general an *increase* in the poverty rate for persons. And in the UK, the government's decision to make the household the unit of analysis in its new statistical series concerned with households below average incomes has been attacked, as likely to underestimate the numbers of people in poverty (CPAG, 1988).

As far as spouses and children are concerned, it is common to use a set of equivalence scales, in order to make a realistic judgement as to how many adult equivalents are having to manage on a particular income. More difficult to judge is the situation of young adults still living with their parents; and old people living with their adult children. In all these cases, however, little can be done to take account, for example, of intra-household inequalities in the control and use of resources, even though these can produce significant differences among members of households in their risk of being, in Townsend's words, 'deprived of enjoying the benefits and participating in the activities customary in that society'.

The assumptions and choices which the investigator makes in regards to these issues in one society may, of course, require modification in regards to another society. Again, therefore, the development of a harmonised system of Community statistics should ideally be such as to permit the application of a variety of different assumptions, the stability of the results being of interest in itself.

4.7 POVERTY IN SPACE AND TIME

If it is sometimes appropriate to focus upon households rather than individuals, it is also sometimes relevant to focus upon the population of whole areas rather than upon individual households. This is, for example, the case where the researcher is investigating dimensions of poverty and disadvantage which are associated with social and economic processes that impinge upon whole areas and which demand an area-focused response; or where it is only data at the level of the area that are available.

Thus, for example, in the United Kingdom, researchers working for the Department of the Environment (DOE) have constructed indicators of the relative levels of deprivation in individual local authorities in England. These indicators include the percentages of unemployed people, overcrowded households lacking exclusive use of basic amenities, pensioners living alone, population change, and a standardised mortality rate. They have been very influential in targeting government resources on the 'most needy' urban areas of England. However, just as measures of poverty which focus on the household risk overlooking intra-household inequalities, so also indicators of area deprivation risk missing sub-area inequalities. The UK government's ranking of local authorities, according to the indicators of deprivation just mentioned, has been widely criticised because when statistics pertaining to still smaller local areas are used, very different conclusions are reached (Flynn, 1986).

In general, the studies reported in this book make little reference to the duration of poverty which people experience; nor to their patterns of movement into and out of poverty. Yet these are, of course, of fundamental importance for the definition of poverty, the development of poverty statistics and the analysis of the causes of poverty. The Schaber studies in Luxembourg have, however, been particularly concerned with these dynamics of poverty (see, for example, Dickes et al., 1980); and the Deleeck studies (to which the Schaber team is contributing), by re-interviewing households at an interval of two years, will also seek to distinguish short-term from longer-term insecurity (Deleeck et al., 1988).

4.8 VISIBLE AND HIDDEN POVERTY

There is, of course, a significant population of the 'hidden poor', who are not included in the population of social assistance recipients because of ignorance or fear of stigma. In Germany, for example, about half of those eligible for social assistance in 1979 did not claim: there were especially high rates of non-claiming in rural areas; among men; among 30–50 year olds; and in southern Germany (Hartmann, 1985). There is no reason to suppose that this declined as a problem during the 1980s.

No less important, many people are missed by household expenditure surveys which 'often exclude information on socio-economic groups of the population for which there is reason to believe that they are affected by poverty. Such groups are, for example, the repatriated immigrants, the political refugees and the illegal alien labour force' (Karantinos, 1987, pp. 1–2). Efforts to improve the comprehensiveness of these statistics are likely to make only slow progress;

and to some extent, they will themselves depend upon the success of policies aimed at reintegrating disadvantaged and excluded groups into the mainstream of society.

Finally, data on various other aspects of disadvantage which are closely associated with poverty also fail to include a significant 'hidden' population. Thus, for example, official data on the numbers of homeless people tend to be limited to those for whom the public authorities have a specific responsibility. In the UK, local authorities have a duty to house families with dependent children, those made homeless by an 'emergency' and those considered 'vulnerable'; and the government statistics for the numbers of homeless in England are based on estimates by local authorities of families housed under this provision. However, single homeless people are rarely eligible under this legislation; and their homelessness therefore remains invisible within the official statistics. To take a very different example, in Greece unemployment data – collected notably through the Commission of the European Communities' Labour Force Survey – 'reflect mainly those unemployed that are seeking wage employment in urban areas' (Karantinos, 1987, p. 40). However, this tends to neglect many of the unemployed and disguised unemployed in rural areas, who are mainly family workers and would-be self-employed, whom the LFS counts as 'employed'. This hidden unemployment is highly correlated with poor living standards (ibid., p. 41).

4.9 POVERTY AND SOCIAL EXCLUSION

Central to Townsend's discussions of poverty has been the social exclusion which is suffered by those who lack even a basic level of resources and rights. With the growth of poverty in the 1980s, researchers and politicians have expressed new fears that where poverty endures over time, and is concentrated into particular spatial areas, the result may be increased 'social exclusion and marginalisation' and 'pathological social behaviour' (Commission of the European Communities, 1988b). Indeed, in the United States, researchers have during the 1980s been giving renewed attention to the 'underclass' that is supposedly developing – and on an increasing scale – in American society.

For the present discussion of concepts and definitions, it must suffice to notice, within this American literature, some of the attempts that have been made to define and measure the 'underclass' that recent processes of social exclusion have allegedly produced. First, its members are said to be suffering – or to face the prospect of – *persistent poverty*. Estimates vary from around 7 per cent of the US population (Sawhill, 1988) to less than 1 per cent (Ruggles and Marton, 1986). Second, they act in ways which are contrary to those of the mainstream of society. They prefer to depend on welfare benefits or illicit earnings, rather than to seek employment. The males eschew stable family relationships. This 'deviant' behaviour is also commonly said to include high rates of school-dropout, teen pregnancy and criminality (Ruggles and Marton, 1986). Third, the members of this underclass are said to be *spatially concentrated*. Ricketts and Sawhill (1986) use census data in order to identify *areas* where the 'deviant' behaviours mentioned above are particularly prevalent. Within the urban areas which they identify, they estimate that around half a million people are members of the underclass, in the sense that they exhibit these 'deviant behaviours'.

Finally, and most contentiously, this behaviour is said by some researchers to be shaped by a specific deviant subculture, through which 'dysfunctional norms or behaviours are transmitted to the next generation . . . hindering the natural process of upward mobility among those who live in the ghetto' (Sawhill, 1986, p. 26). Against this, Wilson seeks to demonstrate that the high rates of crime, etc., in these areas can be accounted for largely in terms of three 'situational' factors: the age composition of the black and Hispanic populations in inner city areas (overwhelmingly young); the high rates of unemployment which they face as a result of changes in the labour market; and their concentration into large, anonymous housing projects/estates, where neighbours are 'less likely to engage in reciprocal guardian behaviour' (Wilson, 1985, p. 152). There is, for Wilson, no need to appeal to inter-generational transmission of pathological behaviour.

The European debates on marginalisation echo a number of these ideas, but without in general endeavouring to derive empirical indicators of the scale and intensity of this exclusion. The final chapter of this book will reassess these American and European debates, in seeking to understand the new patterns of exclusion which the poverty of the 1980s has been producing.

4.10 CONCLUSION

This chapter has provided a brief survey of some of the main definitional and measurement problems in poverty research. Some of these problems are perennial, being associated with more fundamental choices among competing theoretical assumptions and political choices. Even if these conceptual questions can be resolved, however, it will continue to be difficult to make confident assertions about the extent and patterns of poverty in the European Community, in view of the uneven nature of the data which are available for the 12 countries concerned. Nor is it the case that inadequate data availability is a feature of the poorer and southern countries alone. In the case of the Federal Republic of Germany, for example, it is only in respect of social assistance recipients, for the period from 1964 onwards, that we have reasonably good data. Official statistics on unemployment are also good, but data on the income situation of the unemployed are not available. A harmonisation of definitions is therefore a necessary, but is by no means a sufficient condition for rigorous cross-national research into poverty.

5 Recent Trends in Poverty

This chapter will examine what have been the principal trends in the size and composition of the poor population in the countries of the European Community during the 1970s and 1980s. In the course of this discussion, it will be necessary to recall a number of the methodological and conceptual questions raised in the previous chapter. But as will also become quickly apparent, the available data are severely limited and efforts to establish harmonised definitions, for use in Europe-wide research and policy evaluation, are still at an early stage.

5.1 TRENDS IN THE NUMBERS ON SOCIAL ASSISTANCE

We start by considering trends in the numbers of recipients of social assistance. Social assistance schemes act as the final safety net to protect people against destitution. They define the basic minimum standard of living which government declares as the right of its citizens. Social assistance levels of benefit have, therefore, often been taken by researchers and policy-makers as defining the minimum standard of living which is acceptable in the society concerned, especially in those countries where benefit scales are fairly uniform across the country as a whole. These scales are taken as constituting, in effect, an 'official' poverty line. As seen in Section 4.1, there are serious objections to regarding those who receive social assistance – or even those who lie below this level – as the population of the poor. Nevertheless, trends in the numbers of recipients can, at least, indicate the scale on which the public authorities are supporting households on low incomes.

Comparison of social assistance schemes poses difficult methodological problems. As Lawson points out:

> It is generally understood that the social assistance approach is distinguished from other forms of social provision by its subsidiary character and its emphasis on providing benefits only to those who can prove need. Beyond this, however, there is no common agreement as to its precise nature and scope (Lawson, 1979, p. 1).

Some assistance schemes offer primarily financial assistance, as in the UK, the Netherlands and Ireland; some also provide other forms of help such as benefits in kind, medical care, domiciliary aid and social work, as in France, Belgium, Luxembourg, Germany and Denmark (Walker et al., 1984, p. 59).

Some social assistance schemes are specific to particular categories of the population: the elderly, for example, in France and Belgium; other schemes are 'general' in their coverage. In the UK, the employed are excluded from the Income Support scheme (formerly known as Supplementary Benefit): but in many other countries, this is not the case and the numbers of employed people who receive social assistance then gives an indication of those who are on wages which are low relative to their family needs. It is also important to appreciate that the *scale* on which social assistance is used as an element of the social security system varies widely. In the UK, for example, in the mid-1980s the number of recipients corresponded to one in seven families; in Belgium, in contrast, the same period saw fewer than 50 000 recipients of the nationally administered social assistance scheme.

Another important distinction is between centrally and locally organised schemes. The schemes in the UK and Ireland tend to fall into the former category while those in France and Germany, for example, tend to be more locally based (although in France there are a number of national schemes for particular categories of the population, such as the elderly and one parent families). The Dutch and Danish schemes are intermediate in character: although nationally financed and regulated, they leave considerable discretion to local communities in the manner of their implementation. Social assistance schemes at local level can vary substantially, according to local social and political conditions, and benefit levels themselves may vary widely. The existence of a large number of social assistance schemes for particular categories of people means that it is difficult in many countries to establish agreement on national poverty lines.

Table 5.1 reveals that despite the marked differences between schemes, dependence on social assistance has been rising rapidly in the majority of EC countries since 1970. In many countries the number of persons, families or households receiving social assistance has doubled since the beginning of the 1970s. Particularly sharp increases have been recorded in Germany (200 per cent increase in the period 1970–86 in the numbers of households receiving social assistance) and in Belgium (where the number of recipients of the

Minimex or 'Right to a Subsistence Minimum' rose from 9436 in 1976 to 43 774 in 1986). However, this growing dependence on social assistance means that non-take-up of benefits is also of growing importance. This seems to result from the complexity of many countries' social assistance schemes, as well as the stigma and discomfort which are often associated with applying for means-tested benefits.

Some of the schemes indicated in Table 5.1 are restricted to particular categories of the population. In the case of the schemes for the elderly, there has in Belgium been only a modest increase in the number of recipients (12 per cent over the period 1975–86). In Italy – although this is not included in the table – the number of recipients of subsidised minimum pensions – i.e. pensions which are subsidised in order to bring them up to the minimum rates – has been growing steadily, although it is difficult to say how much of this is due to increasing need and how much to enlargement of the range of subsidies (Italian Commission on Poverty, 1985, pp. 335–6). The multiple systems of entitlement make interpretation of the recent trends difficult. In France, however, as the table shows, there has been a substantial decline in the number of recipients of the FNS benefit, despite the fact that the real value of this benefit – and the income threshold below which elderly people are eligible to receive it – has been regularly raised.

In contrast, the API scheme for single parent families in France shows a rising number of recipients. This should, however, be interpreted with care. On the one hand, the benefit is payable for a limited period only, with the aim of supporting such parents during the initial period of single parenthood only. Second, the introduction of this benefit in 1976 means that at least some of the increase in the number of recipients during the subsequent few years may be attributable to gradual diffusion of information about the benefit, rather than to growing numbers of low income, single parent families.

In France and Belgium, as well as in the Mediterranean countries, there are insufficient data to estimate the numbers of recipients of local social assistance, without the risk of double-counting or omissions. Given, however, that in France much of the political pressure for the introduction, in 1988, of a minimum guaranteed income (RMI) came from those responsible for the administration of these local schemes (see Section 2.3), it is worth noticing that the studies which were undertaken in preparation for the introduction of the RMI estimated that about 3 per cent of the population

Table 5.1 Social assistance in EC countries

Country	*1970–74*	*1975–78*	*1979–82*	*1983–87*	*% increase overall*
Belgium RSM (recipients)	–	9,436 (1976)	25,135 (1981)	43,774 (1986)	+363
GIE recipients (elderly)	–	71,875 (1975)	62,757 (1980)	80,294 (1986)	+12
Denmark (families)	150,689 (1972)	236,116 (1977)	289,512 (1980)	300,816 (1983)	+100
France FNS recipients (elderly)	2,178,955 (1972)	2,120,765 (1976)	1,864,811 (1980)	1,557,937 (1987)	−29
(one-parent families: API)	–	40,000 (1978)	70,194 (1982)	114,173 (1986)	+185
Germany (households)	424,134 (1970)	716,803 (1978)	908,104 (1982)	1,270,263 (1986)	+200
Ireland (recipients)	190,400 (1971)	238,900 (1976)	266,000 (1982)	335,200 (1987)	+76
Netherlands (recipients)	299,000 (1970)	429,000 (1975)	384,000 (1980)	606,000 (1985)	+102
UK (families)			2,590,000 (1979)	4,110,000 (1985)	+59

NOTES

Belgium:

Definitions: figures refer to recipients of the 'Right to a Subsistence Minimum' (Minimex), which is a nationally guaranteed social assistance scheme. The figures do not include recipients of locally administered social assistance schemes.

Source: Lammertijn and Luyten (1987).

Denmark:

Definitions: the figures refer to locally administered social assistance, which is in general granted only to people who are not entitled to any other State benefit. Legislative changes in 1977 mean that the figures quoted for 1972 are not strictly comparable with those for the later years.

Source: Danmarks Statistik (ed.) (1986).

France:

Definitions: FNS: if the resources of a pensioner are below a given level, an assistance-type payment is made by the Fonds National de Solidarité. This payment is a supplementary or national 'social minimum' payment. FNS is payable to those aged 65 and above (60 in the case of those unable to work because of invalidity).
API: the 'Allocation de Parent Isolé' was introduced in 1976. This provides a guaranteed minimum income for all lone parents

responsible for looking after any children aged three or less, and pregnant women left alone. Figures refer to beneficiaries.
Source: Ministère des Affaires Sociales et de l'Emploi (1988).

Germany:
Definitions: Social Assistance refers to 'Laufende Hilfe zum Lebensunterhalt', administered by local authorities.
Source: Statistisches Bundesamt (1970ff).

Ireland:
Definitions: Social Assistance here includes supplementary welfare allowances, family income supplement and rent allowance, along with a variety of schemes for particular groups, including unemployment assistance; non-contributory pensions for widows and orphans; assistance for deserted wives, unmarried mothers and prisoners' wives.
Source: Irish Commission on Social Welfare (1986); Department of Social Welfare (1987).

Netherlands:
Definitions: figures refer to the ABW benefit (General Social Assistance Scheme) and RWW benefit (Unemployment Assistance) combined.
Source: Central Bureau of Statistics (1987).

United Kingdom:
Definitions: families in receipt of Supplementary Benefit or housing benefit supplement.
Source: Department of Health and Social Security (1986, 1988b).

(approximately 1.5 million people) would be eligible for this benefit, even though its level is lower than such benefits as API and FNS.

5.2 TRENDS IN THE NUMBERS OF THE POOR

Within many of the countries of the Community, the research community has developed particular tools for defining poverty, taking into account on the one hand the necessities of physical existence and, on the other, the patterns of consumption which are normal in the society concerned. They have then counted the numbers of the population who by these definitions are poor. As seen in Chapter 4, however, the poverty lines defined by the research community are many and varied, testifying perhaps to continuing conceptual confusion over the use of the term 'poverty'. This is, no doubt, one of the reasons for the underdevelopment of comparative poverty statistics.

Some of the financial poverty lines which have been used by official statisticians and social researchers are defined, partly or entirely, by reference to the social assistance scales or other social minimum benefits. Unlike the figures discussed in Section 5.1, however, they include estimates of the numbers of people who, although not receiving social assistance, are at such a low level of income that they are eligible to do so; and in some cases they also include people who are within a certain distance above the social assistance or social minimum levels.

Thus, for example, in the Netherlands, the government's Social and Cultural Planning Office defines a poverty line or minimum in terms of social assistance levels of benefit, with special corrections for the costs of children. Using this line, the percentage of households in poverty increased from 8.4 per cent in 1977 to 10.6 per cent in 1982 (Kapteyn et al., 1985). Researchers at the University of Tilburg, using a slightly modified version of this poverty line, estimate a rise in the poverty rate from 8.1 per cent in 1982 to 9.0 per cent in 1985. But according to these same researchers, this rise would have been even greater had not the levels of minimum benefits suffered, and hence this 'official' poverty line been deflated.

In the United Kingdom, although the government does not define any official poverty line, until recently it published statistics of 'low income families'. These statistics indicated the trends in the numbers of families who are receiving supplementary benefit or housing benefit; and the numbers of families who, although not receiving such benefits, have incomes below supplementary benefit level, or below 110, 120 or 140 per cent of that level. Whichever of these levels is chosen, the official data show that the numbers of 'low income families' increased by one third or more between 1979 and 1983; as a proportion of the overall population they also increased substantially. Between 1983 and 1985, however, this growth was partially reversed. Thus the proportion of persons living on incomes below supplementary benefit level (and thus below the level at which the UK government would have considered their basic needs to have been met) increased from 4 per cent of the population in 1979 to 5.2 per cent in 1983, but then dropped back to 4.5 per cent in 1985; while the proportion living below 140 per cent of supplementary benefit level increased from 22.0 to 30.5 per cent of the population during the same period, falling back to 28.5 per cent in 1985. Nevertheless, the number of persons and families thus defined by some commentators as living in poverty clearly depends on the changing levels of social assistance benefit; and a fierce controversy has raged during recent years over the extent to which the increasing numbers of 'low income families' during the 1980s can be explained in terms of increases in the real value of social assistance benefits (CPAG, 1988, p. 8). The government's recent decision to abandon this statistical series, made in part because of these difficulties in interpreting trends, has been similarly controversial, despite the merits of the new statistical series on 'households below average income' which has been put in its place (Department of Health and Social Security, 1988a).

The poverty lines used in the aforementioned studies are all defined, at least partly, by reference to social minimum schemes which governments have established. However, the most systematic recent estimates of the numbers of poor people in the European Community, which are provided by O'Higgins and Jenkins (1989), have a different conceptual basis. Their study was undertaken in 1987 at the request of the Commission of the European Communities. At the request of the Commission, O'Higgins and Jenkins adopted the definition of poverty which had been used in earlier estimates conducted under Commission auspices (Commission of the European Communities, 1981): the poor are taken as being those households where the disposable income is less than 50 per cent of the average disposable income in the country concerned. For this purpose, they used the equivalence scale proposed by OECD in its publications on social indicators: the first adult in the household has a weight of 1.0; each other adult a weight of 0.7; and each child a weight of 0.5. As they themselves point out, the income data which are available are of varying quality; and for several countries, it was necessary to engage in extrapolation from earlier years, in those cases where data for the mid-1980s were not yet available.

Their study reveals that over the 12 countries of the Community, the number of people in poverty increased slightly, from about 38.6 million around 1975 to 39.5 million around 1980 but then jumped to approximately 43.9 million in 1985. Over the ten years, this involved a rise in the poverty rate from 12.8 to 13.9 per cent. Within these global totals, the highest rates of poverty are to be found in the poorest countries – Greece, Portugal, Ireland and Spain – with between a fifth and a quarter of their populations living in poverty in the mid-1980s. It is, in other words, in these poorest countries that the highest rates of inequality, at least as judged by this relative poverty line, are to be found. There is little sign that these high rates of poverty have been declining during the 1980s. One implication is that during the period of the completion of the Single Market, it will be important to monitor not only whether the peripheral areas of the Community are losing out to the central areas, but also whether, within these peripheral areas, the already large income inequalities are further worsening.

At the opposite extreme, it is in the Benelux countries that the lowest rates of poverty are to be found, with their poverty rates below 8 per cent throughout the period. The UK, Germany and Italy also managed to keep their poverty rates below the average for the twelve countries, although by the mid-1980s both the UK and Italy were moving up towards this average. France and, perhaps surprisingly, Denmark remained above the average.

O'Higgins and Jenkins were also able to examine, to some extent, how this picture would change if the chosen poverty line had been taken as 40 or 60 per cent of average disposable income. 'The most common pattern across countries was that the use of a 40 per cent rather than a 50 per cent line reduced by between two-fifths and one half the proportion of the population in poverty.' A similar *increase* in the proportion in poverty is found when a 60 per cent line is used. These major variations in the size of the poor population mean that 'in research and policy terms, this puts a considerable premium on establishing whether any one of these lines represents a sharp break in the extent to which individuals can participate in the society in which they live' (as Townsend would argue: see Section 4.4 above). If so, this would tend to justify the choice of this line as the poverty line; if not, O'Higgins and Jenkins point out, 'the successively lower levels simply represent bands of increasing deprivation'.

The study by O'Higgins and Jenkins involved a working definition of poverty in terms which are relative to the standard of living of the country concerned; and the choice of this definition is, of course, a matter for legitimate political and scholarly dispute, as the discussion in Chapter 4 revealed. Other definitions generate somewhat different trends. Thus, for example, one of the conceptual debates which were discussed in Chapter 4 (cf. Section 4.3) was concerned with 'absolute' and 'relative' definitions of poverty. In Ireland, Roche has used what was, in effect, an absolute poverty line: 140 per cent of the lowest rate of Unemployment Assistance in 1973, revalued in 1980 to take account of inflation (Roche, 1984). Using this definition, applied to the Household Budget Surveys of 1973 and 1980, he found that the number of adults in poverty fell from 18.8 per cent of the population in 1973 to 10.9 per cent in 1980; the corresponding figures for persons in poverty were 21 and 13.4 per cent.

This is a particularly striking fall, given that the number of unemployed in Ireland doubled between 1971 and 1981 from 76 000 to 141 000. It can be attributed to government policy in respect of income maintenance, for there was a significant increase in real terms in the rates of income maintenance payments during this period (Roche, 1984). Nevertheless, these figures contrast sharply with the stability in the poverty rate for Ireland during this period according to O'Higgins and Jenkins, for persons if not households, using their relative poverty line. In the 1980s, however, when, unlike the 1970s, general living standards – and hence the real value of relative poverty lines – were falling, Nolan and Callan (1989) have shown that a poverty line of the sort that Roche uses produces a larger rise in the numbers of poor than does a 'relative' poverty line.

The new statistical series which the UK government has begun to publish, concerned with households below average income, aims to provide a distributional range rather than to use a single threshold or cut-off level of income. However, it can be used to demonstrate the different results achieved by using poverty lines which are fixed in real terms, rather than moving with the general level of incomes (Department of Health and Social Security, 1988c). A poverty line held constant at 50 per cent of average income in 1981 produces the estimate of 8.3 per cent of persons poor in 1981, falling to 6.7 per cent in 1985. However, a 50 per cent poverty line which, like that employed by O'Higgins and Jenkins, is allowed to move in line with average incomes, produces the estimate of a *rise* in the proportion in poverty, to 9.2 per cent in 1985.

Another of the conceptual debates mentioned in Chapter 4 (Section 4.5) was the choice between 'objective' and 'subjective' poverty lines. In Belgium, researchers at the University of Antwerp have used various 'quasi-subjective' poverty lines to investigate poverty trends in Flanders. One set of lines ('insecurity of subsistence') is based in part on the answers of respondents to the question whether they consider themselves to be in 'insecurity of subsistence'. The second set of lines ('poverty') is set at 75 per cent of the level of the first set (cf. Deleeck et al., 1988). Using these lines, the Antwerp team has shown that the number of households suffering 'insecurity of subsistence' fell from 23.6 per cent of the population in 1976 to 20.9 per cent in 1985; the number of 'poor' households fell from 7.7

per cent to 6.1 per cent over the same period. However, the use of quasi-subjective poverty lines may mean that the recorded decline in the proportion of households who are insecure or poor is in part the result of people's declining expectations, in hard economic times. Certainly the O'Higgins and Jenkins estimates, using their non-subjective poverty line, gives a more modest decline in the rate of poverty for Belgium (or again, more strictly, Flanders), from 7.9 per cent in 1976 to 7.2 per cent in 1985.

5.3 THE CHANGING COMPOSITION OF THE POOR AND OF SOCIAL ASSISTANCE RECIPIENTS

The previous sections of this chapter were concerned with trends in the overall numbers of poor people in the Community. This section will be concerned with the *composition* of this poor population and of the population receiving social assistance; the next section will consider the *incidence* of poverty among specific groups of the population and the extent to which different population groups are dependent on social assistance. 'Poverty' will be defined in terms of low incomes: for it is here that *some* systematic data are available. Nevertheless, as the discussion in Chapter 4 emphasised, there are considerable theoretical as well as methodological limitations to such a definition.

Unfortunately, the study by O'Higgins and Jenkins does not provide composition and incidence data. It will therefore be necessary to rely on data which, because it lacks any standardised definition between countries, is of only limited use in comparative study, but which can, nevertheless, illuminate some of the common trends which have been taking place in the distribution of poverty and in dependence on social assistance.

As seen in the previous sections of this chapter, there are considerable differences between countries in the numbers of the poor and in the numbers of those on social assistance. Nevertheless, Tables 5.2 and 5.3 reveal that the main changes in the composition of the poor and the composition of those on social assistance have been remarkably similar between countries.

There have been two main changes: a substantial *decline* in the proportion of the poor and those on social assistance who are *elderly*; and a sharp *increase* in the proportions who are *unemployed*. In the UK, for example, the declining significance of the elderly among the population of the poor during 1979–85 is evident for three of the four poverty lines given in Table 5.2 (although this decline was to some extent reversed at the end of this period). In Germany, 40 per cent of households receiving social assistance were elderly in 1970 but only 13 per cent in 1986. During the same period the percentage of households receiving social assistance in Germany because of 'loss of employment' rose from 0.7 to 32.7 per cent. In the UK, the percentage of families on social assistance who were unemployed rose from 14.7 to 37.5 per cent between 1979 and 1985. Similar trends can be identified in Table 5.2 for Ireland and in Table 5.3 for Belgium, Ireland and the Netherlands. Greece is the principal exception (Table 5.2). There, the improvement in pensions provisions appears not to have kept pace with the growth in the numbers of the elderly – a demographic trend which Greece shares with the other EC countries – leaving the elderly as a growing proportion of the poor population.

Despite the decline in the proportion of the poor who are elderly, Tables 5.2 and 5.3 reveal that elderly people remain in many countries the largest single category who are poor or on social assistance or, at least, a more significant group than the unemployed. Moreover, even though they have generally declined as a *proportion* of the poor, their absolute numbers have increased in some countries. For example, in the UK the actual number of elderly persons who receive social assistance has remained stable. In 1971 1 865 000 pensioners claimed supplementary benefit compared to 1 875 000 in 1986–87 who received supplementary benefit or housing benefit supplement. In Ireland, the number of elderly persons receiving social assistance increased between 1971 and 1987 from 113 600 to 124 400, even though the proportion of those on social assistance who were elderly fell from 59.7 to 37.1 per cent (Table 5.3).

Another important change in the composition of the poor, particularly in some of the more rural countries such as Italy, Greece and Portugal, is that the percentage of the poor who belong to large families seems to be declining. In Italy 38.4 per cent of poor families had five or more members in 1983 compared to almost 60 per cent in 1983; in Greece, between 1974 and 1981/2, the proportion declined from almost 46 to 40 per cent; while in Portugal, 16.6 per cent of households in absolute poverty were large in 1980 compared to 29.6 per cent in 1973/4 (see Table 5.2). Given that there was no substantial increase in poverty in these three countries during this period, it would seem that the actual number of poor large families had also

Table 5.2 The composition of the poor population (percentages)

Population group	*Greece*		*Ireland households*					*Italy persons*		*Portugal households*		*United Kingdom*							
												persons				*individuals*			
			absolute poverty		*relative poverty*							*poverty*		*margins of poverty*		*absolute poverty*		*relative poverty*	
	1974	*1981/2*	*1973*	*1980*	*1973*	*1980*	*1987*	*1978*	*1983*	*1973/4*	*1980*	*1979*	*1985*	*1979*	*1985*	*1981*	*1985*	*1981*	*1985*
Elderly (aged 65+)	28.0	32.2	10.3	8.0	–	–	10.7	–	21.8	–	31.0	53.1	39.7	50.9	36.1	11.9	10.0	11.9	12.7
Large families (2 parents and 3 or more children)	45.9	40.1	–	20.5	14.6	20.0	25.6	59.6	38.4	29.6	16.6	8.6	10.3	15.0	15.3	–	–	–	–
Employed	17.6	14.6	57.0	52.0	–	–	13.2	–	–	56.0	35.0	22.5	23.1	20.7	18.8	24.0	18.6	24.0	20.3
Unemployed	29.2	25.0	12.5	23.1	–	15.0	32.7	–	–	–	–	7.2	21.1	9.9	24.3	43.5	52.0	43.5	49.4
Single people	28.7	20.1	–	–	27.6	21.8	9.1	8.9	8.4	5.8	11.3	17.2	22.7	8.7	15.6	9.8	14.4	9.8	14.5

NOTES:

Greece:

Definitions: large families: six members or more.
Employed: wage or salary earner (excludes self-employed).

Source: National Centre for Social Research (1990).

Ireland:

Definitions: the data for trends in absolute poverty between 1973 and 1980 are taken from Roche (1984); the data for relative poverty trends are taken from Combat Poverty Agency (1988) and Nolan (1987), whose definition of poverty is that of O'Higgins and Jenkins (1989). For discussion of both definitions, see para. 5.3 of the text.

Sources: Roche (1984); Combat Poverty Agency (1988); Nolan (1987).

Italy:

Definitions: large families: families with six or more members. The Commission on Poverty used a relative poverty line similar to that used by O'Higgins and Jenkins (1989) and the European Commission (1981): see Section 5.3 of text.

Source: Italian Commission on Poverty (1985).

Portugal:

Definitions: da Costa and Silva use an 'absolute poverty' line, applied to data in the Household Income and Expenditure Surveys of 1973/4 and 1980, undertaken by the National Institute of Statistics. They use an age-related equivalence scale. Large families are here defined as those with more than four adult equivalents. The figure for the employed refers in 1973/4 to urban households only; in 1980 to both urban and rural; the figures are therefore not strictly comparable. Except for the row 'large families', all figures refer to heads of households.

Source: da Costa et al. (1985).

United Kingdom:

Definitions: Column 1: 'Poverty': Figures are for persons in families with relative net resources below the level of supplementary benefit (including housing benefit supplement) but not receiving it.

Column 2: 'Margins of Poverty': Figures are for persons in families who are receiving supplementary benefit or housing benefit supplement *plus* those with relative net resources below 140 per cent of the level of supplementary benefit (including housing benefit supplement).

Column 3: 'Absolute Poverty': Percentage of individuals below 50 per cent of the 1981 real terms population average income (before housing costs).

Column 4: 'Relative Poverty': Percentage of individuals below 50 per cent of the current year population average income (before housing costs).

Source: Columns 1 and 2: Department of Health and Social Security (1986, 1988b).
Columns 3 and 4: Department of Health and Social Security (1988c, Tables B1, B2, C1, C2).

NOTES (i) The figures in Columns 3 and 4, based on the new statistical series for 'household below average income' (see discussion in Section 5.2 of text), involve a distinctive set of equivalence scales, for households of different composition. It is difficult to say how far the divergence between the trends revealed in Columns 1 and 2, and those in Columns 3 and 4, arises from these equivalisation procedures.

(ii) It may be misleading to refer to the definition used in Column 3 as an 'absolute' poverty line because there, as in Column 4, the threshold is defined with reference to average disposable income rather than, for example, to any calculation of basic needs. Nevertheless, it is absolute rather than relative in the sense that as average disposable incomes change, the threshold is kept fixed, by reference to real income levels in the base year (here 1981).

Table 5.3 The Composition of Those Receiving or Reliant on Social Assistance (percentages)

Population group	*Belgium recipients*		*Germany households*			*Ireland recipients*		*Netherlands persons*		*United Kingdom families*		
	1976	*1986*	*1970*	*1980*	*1986*	*1971*	*1987*	*1970*	*1985*	*1979*	*1983*	*1985*
Elderly (aged 65+)	12.5	4.9	40.0	22.0	13.0	59.7	37.1	28.0	1.5	65.0	44.0	39.4
Large families (2 parents and 3 or more children)	–	–	1.9	1.9	2.5	–	–	–	–	4.2	5.5	5.6
Unemployed	–	–	0.7	10.5	32.7	22.5	45.8	2.7	66.7	14.7	35.4	37.5
Single parents	–	–	13.6	17.7	17.0	–	–	32.0	21.0	12.4	12.6	13.1
								(*1981*)	(*1984*)			
Sick invalids	–	–	–	8.7	6.1	–	–	–	–	6.5	4.7	5.4
Single people	65.0	63.0	–	66.0	63.0	–	–	–	–	15.0	27.5	30.4

NOTES:
Definitions and sources: see notes to Table 5.1
Germany: figures for the employed are for recipients not households. For the unemployed, the figures for 1985 are not strictly comparable with those for the earlier years.

decreased. These countries seem to be moving towards the pattern in countries such as Germany and the UK, where only a very small proportion of the poor and those on social assistance belong to large families. At the same time, it is worth noticing that in those two northern countries these proportions have been rising somewhat over this period. A similar – but more dramatic – increase is evident in Ireland, as Table 5.2 reveals. As Nolan (1987) has commented: 'whereas the average number of persons per household . . . fell [between 1973 and 1980] the average size of "poor" households either rose or fell only marginally (depending on the poverty line used) between the two years'.

In some countries, including the UK and Portugal, an increasing proportion of the poor and those on social assistance are single. However, it is not clear from the data that are available what are the characteristics of these people and to what extent they might be young unemployed individuals, the elderly (particularly women living alone), single low-paid workers, etc. The opposite trend is evident in Greece and Ireland, however, and to some extent in Belgium and Germany, and there is no clear picture for the Community countries as a whole.

Table 5.3 reveals a similarly mixed pattern as far as single parent families are concerned. In Germany and the UK, there has been some increase in their representation among social assistance recipients; and in France there has been substantial growth in the numbers of API recipients (see Table 5.1). In the Netherlands, however, the opposite trend is evident. In Table 5.2, the UK data reveal a variety of different trends depending upon the poverty line and definitions used.

5.4 CHANGES IN THE INCIDENCE OF POVERTY AND IN DEPENDENCE ON SOCIAL ASSISTANCE

Tables 5.4 and 5.5 reveal how the incidence of poverty or dependence on social assistance has changed for particular population groups.

The figures indicate that as well as a decline in the proportion of the poor who are elderly, there has also been a decline in the risk or likelihood of the elderly being poor or having to rely on social assistance. The figures for Ireland, Belgium, France, Greece and the United Kingdom show this clearly. In France, as already noted, the decline in dependence on social assistance has taken place despite

Table 5.4 The incidence of poverty among various population groups (percentages)

Population group	*Belgium households*				*Greece households*		*Ireland households*				*Italy persons*		*Netherlands households*		*Portugal households*		*United Kingdom persons*				*United Kingdom individuals*			
	insecurity of subsistence		*poor*				*absolute poverty*		*relative poverty*								*poverty*		*margins of poverty*		*absolute poverty*		*relative poverty*	
	1976	*1985*	*1976*	*1985*	*1974*	*1981/2*	*1973*	*1980*	*1980*	*1987*	*1978*	*1983*	*1982*	*1985*	*1973/4*	*1980*	*1979*	*1985*	*1979*	*1985*	*1981*	*1985*	*1981*	*1985*
Elderly (aged 65+)	40.0	35.4	15.0	11.1	35.8	31.2	30.3	12.9	19.7	8.4	–	–	–	–	–	54.0	12.7	10.6	67.5	61.3	6.0	4.0	6.0	7.0
Large families (5 or more members)	–	–	–	–	45.9	40.1	–	20.0	–	–	18.4	18.7	10.9	5.3	66.0	71.5	2.6	4.2	24.7	39.6	–	–	–	–
Employed	14.0	10.5	3.0	1.5	17.6	14.6	15.0	9.0	–	–	–	–	2.7	1.2	–	–	1.2	1.7	6.2	8.7	3.0	2.0	3.0	3.0
Unemployed	51.0	60.1	27.0	28.8	29.2	25.0	67.0	61.0	67.8	59.9	–	–	36.5	28.3	–	–	12.1	12.1	91.9	88.9	42.0	36.0	42.0	47.0
Single parent families	–	–	–	–	–	–	–	19.0	–	–	–	–	18.2	12.2	–	–	4.5	3.4	54.0	73.7	18.0	11.0	18.0	15.0
Single	–	–	–	–	28.7	20.1	–	–	–	–	15.8	15.5	14.8	17.5	22.2	38.4	4.7	5.3	13.3	23.2	5.0	5.0	5.0	7.0
Sick/disabled	49.0	43.8	21.0	15.7	–	–	57.0	40.0	–	–	–	–	36.8	19.8	–	–	4.3	4.2	41.1	45.8	21.0	16.0	21.0	19.0
Overall incidence of poverty	23.6	20.9	7.7	6.1	25.0	20.6	21.0	13.4	17.2	18.9	10.6	11.1	8.1	9.0	36.0	35.0	4.0	4.5	22.0	28.5	8.3	6.7	8.3	9.2

NOTES:
Belgium:
Definitions: figures refer to Flanders only. Poverty lines have been developed by a research team at the University of Antwerp. For details, see Section 5.3 of text.
Source Cantillon et al. (1987); Bergham et al. (1985).

Greece:
Sources and definitions: see notes to Table 5.2.

Ireland:
Sources and definitions: see notes to Table 5.2.

Italy:
Sources and definitions: see notes to Table 5.2.

Netherlands:
Definitions: the poverty line defined by the government's Social and Cultural Planning Office (discussed in text, para. 5.3), but somewhat modified by University of Tilburg researchers.
Source: research currently under way at the University of Tilburg.

Portugal:
Definitions: figures for the elderly refer to those aged 75 or more. Figures for large families refer to those with more than five adult equivalents. Except for the row 'large families', all figures refer to heads of households.
Source: see notes to Table 5.2.

United Kingdom:
Sources and definitions: see notes to Table 5.2.

Table 5.5 The proportion of various population groups who receive social assistance (percentages)

Population group	*France persons*			*Germany households*				*United Kingdom families*		
	1972	*1980*	*1987*	*1972*	*1980*	*1985*		*1979*	*1983*	*1985*
Elderly (aged 65+)	32.5	24.8	20.8	–	1.8	1.5	(60–75)	26.2	24.2	24.3
				–	2.6	2.3	(75+)			
Single parent families	–	–	–	4.8	8.6	11.3		37.6	48.4	59.3
				1975	*1980*	*1985*				
Unemployed	–	30.0	38.0	13.9	24.3	32.7		62.3	55.8	67.0
Proportion of the total population who receive social assistance	–	–	–	–	3.1	4.4		10.0	13.0	14.3

NOTES:
France:
Sources and definitions: see notes to Table 5.1; and INSEE (1987).
Germany:
Definitions: figures for the elderly refer to recipients not households. Figures for the unemployed refer to those who lack any entitlement to unemployment insurance or unemployment assistance and who are, at most, eligible for local social assistance.
Source: see notes to Table 5.1.
United Kingdom:
Sources and definitions: see notes to Table 5.1.

regular increases in the real value of this categorical benefit. It is worth adding that around 40 per cent of the recipients are former farm workers: their dependence on social assistance testifies to the low level of wages in the agricultural sector, but with the decline in the proportion of the labour force in that sector, continuing falls in the use of the FNS benefit may be expected. Nevertheless, at least in Belgium and Greece, the risk of poverty for the elderly remains higher than that for the population as a whole; the same is true of the United Kingdom, at least in relation to the older series of statistics on 'low income families'.

For the unemployed, trends in the risk of poverty or of dependence on social assistance vary considerably. Thus in Belgium, France and Germany, in the period until the mid-1980s, their situation appears to have worsened. In Ireland and the Netherlands, the situation seems to have improved during the same period. In the United Kingdom the evidence of Tables 5.4 and 5.5 is inconclusive. The Greek data, indicating a declining risk of poverty for the unemployed, are for a somewhat earlier period, before the era of high rates of unemployment.

There has been a sharp rise in reliance on social assistance by single parent households in countries such as Germany and the United Kingdom. (In France, it is probably not very meaningful to ask what proportion of single parent families receive the API benefit, since the latter benefit is for a limited duration only, intended to ease the initial period of single parenthood and to support re-entry to the labour market by single mothers.) As to the incidence of poverty among single parent families, Table 5.4 indicates that this fell, at least in the Netherlands and the UK, during the first half of the 1980s. Nevertheless, the figures support O'Higgins' conclusion that the members of these families are much more likely than others to fall into the lower income groups (O'Higgins, 1987). However, he also emphasises the heterogeneity of the circumstances of such families, and the variations between countries in their risk of finding themselves at particular levels of low income. From Table 5.4, it is, moreover, clear that in the UK at least, the extent to which the risk of poverty for single parent families exceeds that for the general population depends heavily upon the definition of poverty which is used.

Finally, in Portugal and Italy traditional poverty associated with large family size is declining but among those large families that remain, a larger proportion are poor than was the case in the 1970s. However, the risk level is also increasing in the United Kingdom.

5.5 CONCLUSION

Despite the limitations placed on this discussion by data availability and comparability, it is clear that the 1980s have seen significant changes in the extent and distribution of poverty within the populations of the European Community countries. It is also evident that these developments are linked to changes in the labour market, in the family and in systems of social protection, but that significant variations are to be found between the richer and the less developed countries. The next four chapters of this book will seek to make sense of these various factors and to examine the responses which governments have made.

6 Poverty, Unemployment and the Labour Market

6.1 INTRODUCTION

It is the sharp rise in unemployment since the 1970s, together with associated changes in the labour market, that has been the most important influence on the restructuring of poverty (see Section 5.4 above).

The growth in unemployment is a result of changes in the working population and in the number of jobs available. Changes in the working population are due to the fall in the number of young people entering the labour force, the progressive increase in the female labour force participation rate and the increasing rates of early retirement (or declining rates of labour force participation among older workers). Some of these trends are summarised in Tables 6.1–6.2. They have helped to produce a modest net increase in the working population of the 12 Community countries during the 1970s and 1980s, which rose from 127.12 million in 1970 to 140.80 million in 1986 (Commission of the European Communities, 1988a, table III), although as a proportion of those of working age, there has been little change and the total participation ratio has remained close to 64 per cent during the 1970s and 1980s (Commission of the European Communities, 1988d, table A8a).

As for the number of jobs, this shows for the EC countries overall something of a reduction in the early 1980s, followed by a revival during the subsequent years (OECD, 1988b, table 1.2). The net result is that unemployment, having risen dramatically during the 1970s and the early 1980s, has since then dropped somewhat in most

Table 6.1 Female labour force participation ratios (percentages)

	1975	*1979*	*1982*	*1985*	*1986*
European Community of 12 countries	45.3	47.0	47.8	49.0	50.0

Definitions: Female labour force as per cent of female population of working age (15–64).
Source: Commission of the European Communities (1988d), table A8b.

Table 6.2 Labour force participation rates of workers aged 55–64 (percentages)

Country	*1960–70*	*1971–80*	*1981–85*
France	59.3 (1960)	51.5 (1975)	40.1 (1985)
Germany	52.9 (1962)	42.4 (1975)	38.4 (1985)
Ireland	55.6 (1961)	52.4 (1975)	47.3 (1984)
Italy	37.4 (1960)	24.7 (1975)	23.5 (1984)
Netherlands	–	42.2 (1975)	35.2 (1984)
Portugal	–	53.4 (1975)	49.5 (1984)
Spain	–	48.9 (1975)	42.3 (1985)
United Kingdom	58.8 (1960)	62.8 (1975)	49.7 (1985)

Source: OECD Labour Force Statistics.

countries (Table 6.3); Table 6.7 gives unemployment figures on a standardised basis, but only for the most recent years. However, the more recent development in the amount of available employment has been accompanied by a diversification in the types of work, with the increasing incidence of temporary employment, fixed term contracts and part-time work.

Although unemployment has remained at high levels, this development has not had a uniform effect throughout the whole working population. The most marked increase in unemployment has been visible among blue-collar workers, unskilled workers and foreigners, while unemployment among managerial staff, technicians and those holding higher education qualifications has remained fairly stable. At the same time, the average duration of unemployment has also increased considerably (Tables 6.4, 6.5). Whereas, in the 1970s, a period of six months was considered to be a long time, today long-term unemployment covers one or more years. Moreover, the increase in the average period of unemployment in fact covers a dual development: the extension of long-term unemployment and the growing frequency of recurrent unemployment (short-term but repetitive). The former tends to affect such groups as older workers and

Table 6.3 Unemployment rates in the Community (number of unemployed as percentage of civilian labour force, annual averages)

	1973	*1975*	*1979*	*1982*	*1986*	*1987*	*1988*	*1989*
Belgium	2.8	5.1	8.4	13.0	12.6	12.3	11½	11¼
Denmark	0.8	5.0	5.8	9.3	7.4	7.6	8½	8¼
Germany	1.1	4.1	3.3	6.9	8.1	8.1	8	8¼
Greece	–	–	–	5.8	7.4	7.4	7½	7½
Spain	2.6	4.1	8.6	16.4	21.0	20.5	20	19¾
France	1.8	3.9	6.0	8.7	10.7	10.8	10¾	10¾
Ireland	5.5	8.4	7.4	12.3	18.2	19.2	18¾	18¼
Italy	4.9	5.3	6.7	9.7	13.7	14.0	15	14½
Luxembourg	0.0	0.2	0.7	1.3	1.4	1.6	1½	1¼
Netherlands	3.1	5.3	5.5	11.8	12.1	11.5	11¼	11
Portugal	–	–	–	–	8.7	7.2	6½	6½
UK	2.2	3.6	4.7	10.6	12.0	10.6	8½	7¼
EUR 9	2.4	4.3	5.2	9.3	11.1	10.8	10½	10¼
EUR 12	–	–	–	–	11.9	11.6	11¼	11

Definition: for EUR 9 registered unemployed, SOEC definition; for Greece, Spain, Portugal labour force surveys. The figures for 1987, 1988 and 1989 are estimates and forecasts of the Commission services, September/October 1988.

Source: Commission of the European Communities (1988d), Table A1.

women without qualifications; the latter affects, for example, young workers who rotate between unemployment, employment and the special training schemes that have been created for their particular benefit.

The high rate of unemployment during the 1980s, together with associated changes in the labour market, has had a number of major effects on the extent and distribution of poverty in the countries of the European Community. There is, first, clear evidence of significant gaps and limitations in income support and social protection for the unemployed. In addition, however, recent years have also revealed growing disparities of income and welfare between those confined to insecure and low-paid jobs and those who are fortunate enough to remain in relatively stable and secure occupations. It is upon these developments that this chapter will now focus.

6.2 INCOME SUPPORT DURING UNEMPLOYMENT

There is evidence in most countries of widening disparities of income

Table 6.4 Long-term unemployment (as percentage of total unemployment)

	1983	*1984*	*1985*	*1986*
Belgium	64.1	67.1	68.2	69.2
Denmark	32.2	30.9	32.0	26.5
Germany	38.4	43.4	46.9	47.6
Greece	32.3	37.1	43.4	41.8
Spain	52.5	53.4	56.3	58.4
France	39.6	39.1	43.8	44.7
Ireland	35.2	44.5	62.2	62.9
Italy	54.6	60.5	63.6	65.6
Luxembourg	32.7	29.3	36.8	29.0
Netherlands	46.9	–	56.4	–
Portugal	45.2	43.5	48.4	53.4
UK	44.8	45.5	48.7	46.3
EUR 12	46.3	48.3	52.1	52.7

Definition: Continuously unemployed for one year or more.
Source: Commission of the European Communities (1988d), Table A3b.

Table 6.5 Very long-term unemployment (as percentage of total unemployment)

	1983	*1984*	*1985*	*1986*
Belgium	41.8	44.7	51.5	53.5
Denmark	12.3	10.4	13.3	9.6
Germany	14.9	20.2	26.7	29.4
Greece	11.7	14.3	19.5	17.6
Spain	–	–	–	37.3
France	17.7	19.3	21.8	24.0
Ireland	19.7	–	41.1	42.6
Italy	28.0	34.6	38.1	41.3
Luxembourg	14.4	15.9	13.8	13.0
Netherlands	22.3	–	35.7	–
Portugal	–	–	–	32.7
UK	24.8	29.2	33.2	31.7
EUR 12	22.3	26.0	30.9	33.2

Definition: Continuously unemployed for two years or more.
Source: Commission of the European Communities (1988d), Table A3b.

and welfare among different sections of the unemployed. To a large extent these reflect the selectivity which is inherent in unemployment compensation policies. The protection which is provided by unemployment insurance schemes, although it varies considerably between EC countries, is everywhere subject to important restrictions. These restrictions include conditions which link entitlements to previous contribution and employment records; disqualifications from benefit where unemployment is deemed 'voluntary'; and, most important of all, limits on the duration of payments. Only Belgium allows insurance benefits to be drawn for an unlimited period. However, even there, payments are conditional upon a 'decent life style', as well as on daily registration at an employment agency; and those who are unemployed for an abnormally long period (i.e. twice the average redundancy period of the region) may be legally excluded (Vandenbroucke, 1987, p. 40). In Denmark, where conditions of entitlement are generous by European standards, these were made more restrictive in the early 1980s, as the fiscal burden of unemployment benefit grew and as employers insisted that overly generous benefits were having negative effects on work incentives (Abrahamson et al., 1987, p. 10). These restrictions included previous contribution and employment records; reduced opportunity for the unemployed to refuse job offers; and longer qualifying periods for unemployed school leavers (ibid., pp. 10–11).

Moreover, within unemployment insurance, much less progress has been made in developing effective minimum income guarantees than in social security for pensioners or the sick and disabled. Most unemployment insurance schemes contain minimum benefit levels or provisions to increase payments for the lower paid, but their effects are often counteracted by other conditions designed to preserve work incentives. In practice many insurance benefits, especially for the longer-term unemployed, fall below the social minima of the national social assistance scheme.

With such restrictions, unemployment insurance has become, especially in the 1980s, the most limited and selective of all social insurance measures. Indeed, with the rapid growth of recurrent as well as long-term unemployment, and the high rate of unemployment among young people and women who have not been able to build up insurance rights, these insurance provisions are now failing in most EC countries to protect the majority of the unemployed. In practice, therefore, many of the victims of unemployment in the 1980s depend on more basic forms of social assistance, often providing poverty-line benefits, or on support from families or voluntary agencies.

Thus, for example, in the *United Kingdom*, which is often assumed to have created one of the most comprehensive (if not generous) social insurance schemes, the proportion of unemployed men receiving insurance benefits has fallen from 55 per cent in 1971 to 25 per cent in 1987. Out of a total of 2.5 million men and women officially registered as unemployed in 1987, just under 1.4 million persons were dependent for their livelihood on social assistance (the national means-tested Supplementary Benefits scheme).

In *Germany*, the proportion of the unemployed with a claim to unemployment compensation or unemployment assistance fell from 86 per cent in 1975 to 67 per cent in 1985. During this period there has been a rapid growth in the reliance of the unemployed on local social assistance: between 1970 and 1986 the proportion of social assistance recipients reporting unemployment as the reason for their application rose from 1 to 33 per cent.

In *Portugal*, only 11 per cent of the unemployed were receiving unemployment benefit in August 1983, but this percentage has increased in more recent years, with the introduction of a (non-contributory) social subsidy for unemployment and the integration of unemployment benefits into the general social security system.

In both *Denmark* and *the Netherlands* the unemployed now account for more than 60 per cent of those on social assistance. (The great majority are under 30 years of age and many are single persons.)

In *France*, in the mid-1980s, of the unemployed who did not receive benefit, about one third had no entitlement, while a further quarter had exhausted whatever entitlement they had. Levels of unemployment benefit are in general low.

In *Spain*, the proportion of the unemployed receiving unemployment benefit fell during the early 1980s to less than 20 per cent; the introduction of means-tested unemployment assistance has lifted the proportion with a claim to some form of unemployment support to around 30 per cent.

Finally, in *Italy*, 'unemployment compensation practically does not exist' (Brandolini and Razzano, 1987, p. 17). This is a situation not unlike that which prevails in the United States; and it reminds us that the 'European model' of generous welfare provision, distinguishing our own Continent from that of other capitalist societies, was always something of a myth.

6.3 UNEMPLOYMENT AND 'NEW POVERTY'

The summary tables presented in Chapter 5 suggested that in many countries, there has been a sharp rise during the last ten years in the proportion of the poor made up of the unemployed and their dependents (see especially Table 5.2). This to some extent reflects the low level of unemployment benefit in some countries; it also reflects the large numbers of the unemployed who, as seen in the previous section, are not entitled to unemployment benefit and must therefore turn to social assistance or to support from their families and from voluntary agencies. As Table 5.3 revealed, the proportion of social assistance recipients made up of the unemployed and their dependents is therefore also rising.

There appear to be significant variations between countries in the extent to which social assistance has protected the unemployed from poverty. Most countries lack national social security or assistance measures which apply systematic standards to the unemployed as a whole. Some countries, moreover, have failed to raise social assistance benefits in line with inflation. This occurred, for example, in Germany from the late 1970s to the mid-1980s, although recently efforts have been made to compensate for this. In Denmark, similarly, 1982 saw a freeze on various social benefits for the sick and unemployed and on social assistance, with lower benefit levels for long-term recipients of social assistance (Abrahamson et al., 1987, p. 3).

Despite these recent restrictions, minimum social assistance benefits for the unemployed in Denmark remain relatively generous by comparative standards, as they do in the Netherlands also. Even so, there are indications that even here, at least some sections of the unemployed have experienced severe hardship. Morkeberg (1985), for example, studying a sample of the unemployed in Denmark at the turn of the decade, found that three-fifths had experienced some kind of financial hardship during their period of unemployment, being forced to reduce their consumption even of day-to-day necessities. In addition, the bulk of those with savings had been forced to use them for normal consumption; and many had been forced to borrow from family or from credit institutions or to sell assets in order to make ends meet. Since the date of this study, of course, long-term unemployment has become increasingly serious and the financial hardship described here will therefore have tended to worsen (Abrahamson et al., 1987, Appendix A).

In the United Kingdom, the national Supplementary Benefit

scheme (now Income Support) seems to have provided higher standards of support, when related to average incomes, than basic assistance measures for the unemployed in countries such as Germany and France. However, the British scheme involves considerable surveillance and control of the unemployed and, as recent studies have shown, provides at best a barely adequate minimum standard of living. According to the 'Breadline Britain' survey, Supplementary Benefit levels fall considerably below what the majority of people in Britain regarded as a minimum acceptable way of life in the 1980s. Moreover, the survey estimated that in 1983 there were about 1.65 million adults and nearly one million children in poverty as a result of unemployment; of this group nearly half the adults and over half the children were in 'intense poverty' (Mack and Lansley, 1985, p. 187).

Formidable problems have arisen from the shame and stigma still attached in many countries to 'poor relief'. The idea of applying for social assistance has long been anathema to many ordinary workers and their families in countries such as France, Germany and Ireland, much more so than in countries with national or more standardised schemes. Recent German surveys suggest that up to half of all unemployed persons who are eligible for local relief are still not applying, mainly because of feelings of shame. Or, as the President of the Society of St Vincent de Paul in Ireland comments: 'The so-called "new poor" are the most reluctant to come forward . . . and admit that they need help. They are ashamed, embarrassed and just don't know the ropes of the system' (*Irish Press*, 17 March 1987).

Perhaps the most striking evidence of the difficulties of these new poor is the increase in debts, particularly arrears in rents, mortgages and hire purchase and credit arrangements. Repossessions of houses and flats from defaulting owner-occupiers have increased almost ten-fold in the United Kingdom between 1979 and 1986. In Belgium over 700 000 persons in 1985 were subject to official warning procedures for cutting of gas or electricity supplies (although of course many of these may not have been poor), and 65 000 reported severe problems in paying financial debts. A Dutch study estimated that in the mid-1980s 150 000 households could not solve their financial problems because their debts were too high (De Greef and Middel, 1986), while research at one credit bank in north Holland found that 80 per cent of people applying for loans in 1984 were refused because of their financial situation and the majority of these were unemployed.

6.4 WIDER LABOUR MARKET TRENDS AND POVERTY

In examining new aspects of poverty, it is important not to draw too sharp a contrast between the fortunes of the unemployed and employed. Many of those in employment over the past decade have found themselves with low or declining real wages, poor working conditions and job security, and low standards of social assistance and welfare. This is especially true in many of Europe's depressed regions and inner cities, where, as one British study has put it, 'the destinies of the employed and the unemployed are inseparable . . . neither employment nor unemployment is a stable condition . . . unemployment is, more than anything, an intensification of tribulations that are commonplace: powerlessness, low status, low and fluctuating incomes are the lot of the unskilled, the uncertificated, the unorganised, in work or out of it' (Harrison, 1983, p. 109).

There is evidence of growing segmentation or 'dualism' in the labour market, which has rendered precarious the employment of an increasing proportion of the labour force. The existence of a 'secondary labour market' has, of course, long been evident, even in the most advanced and prosperous countries of the European Community; however, until the recession its marginalising effects were most likely to be felt by specific minorities, notably immigrant workers. In the second half of the 1970s, immigration controls and pressures of return migration were important factors in containing unemployment and in reducing the visibility of the problem of precarious employment. This has now changed, with the rapid rise in unemployment and the efforts to re-liberalise and deregulate the economies in a number of countries. In the 1980s, growing numbers of indigenous as well as foreign workers are in the 'secondary market', with a high risk of unemployment, low skills, poor working conditions and weak trade union protection. Many are on temporary or part-time contracts, or in the grey areas of the labour market, where employers can evade social and labour laws. In France, for example, in the mid-1980s almost 1.5 million workers were officially estimated as being in temporary, subcontracted or part-time employment. The number of people involved in training courses and in the TUC programme (community employment) has grown especially fast (75 000 in 1982; 300 000 in 1986). According to French surveys, the number of persons in employment but actively seeking another job has risen from around 500 000 in the early 1970s to 1.4 million in 1986. The main reason for the search for other employment is precarious or under-employment in the job occupied.

Another major cause of concern is the fate of many 'prime-age' workers, particularly manual workers and their families, whose skills have become increasingly obsolescent with the decline in manufacturing. As a recent ILO report (Standing, 1986) observes, to some extent this group has been cushioned over the past decade by union resistance and employment protection legislation. However, during the 1980s many workers 'have become prone to "concession bargaining", conceding employment security for pay rises'. Those adversely affected, including many with long-standing craft skills and a pride in their 'social security', have grown increasingly vulnerable to unemployment and a marked drop in their living standards. As the ILO report puts it, 'many of the new poor come from this traditional backbone of . . . industry'.

Developments like these have not only served to reproduce and reinforce traditional links between low pay and poverty. They have also linked uncertainty of employment more closely than previously with inferior and uncertain forms of social protection; and they help, for example, to explain the recent dramatic erosion of social insurance protection (particularly, but by no means only, unemployment insurance). Finally, they may help to explain why, in Germany for example, the employed make up a growing share of social assistance recipients (up from 0.7 per cent in 1970 to 4.6 per cent in 1985: Statistisches Bundesamt, 1970ff); and in the UK, a growing proportion of those with incomes below Supplementary Benefit level (up from 12.9 per cent in 1979 to 15.0 per cent in 1985: Department of Health and Social Security, 1986, 1988b).

It is also evident that the links between low and erratic pay, job security and poverty remain marked in the poorer regions of the EC. In Italy, where almost a third of the poor belong to the labour force, the risk of poverty is especially high among factory workers and self-employed individuals in the South. At the same time, however, one in six of the poor employed is a clerical or service worker: the working poor are by no means confined to particular sectors of the labour force (Italian Commission on Poverty, 1985: figures for 1983). In Portugal, Spain and Greece high inflation rates have substantially reduced the purchasing power of wages (although in more recent years, inflation has in general decelerated). In Portugal, for example, the proportion of employees among the heads of poor households was 35 per cent in 1980; and in the mid-1980s, 13 per cent of all employees were in temporary jobs, while about half the working poor did not have written contracts of employment. There were also around 100 000 workers whose payment of wages or other benefit was delayed by employers. These figures have dropped somewhat more recently, in part because of the legislative measures taken by the Government in 1985–86; but some of the reduction may well have been due to the closure of some of the firms which had been delaying the payment of wages (Departmento Central de Planeamento, 1986).

The problem of these groups have in some cases been exacerbated by ambivalent and uncertain government policies. Officially, most governments have sought to 'protect' low wage earners, and some, indeed, have laid great stress on the need for low wages to be higher than unemployment benefits, in order to maintain work incentives. In practice, however, the low paid have often been hit even more severely than the unemployed by cuts in social benefits and increasing rent costs and tax changes. This was most notably the case in the United Kingdom in the early part of the 1980s, a period which saw the numbers of low paid workers and their families with incomes at or below Supplementary Benefit level increase by almost half (Department of Health and Social Security, 1986). Significant cuts in the living standards of the low paid in the 1980s appear also to have occurred in the Netherlands, Denmark and Ireland.

6.5 VULNERABLE GROUPS

Unemployment and other recent changes in the labour market, although changing the map of poverty significantly, have also hit particularly hard those groups which were traditionally in a weak position within the labour market, including ethnic minorities, women and the young.

Ethnic minorities have fared badly. In the UK, there is substantial evidence of discrimination in the labour market and of disproportionately high unemployment rates (Department of Employment, 1987). In other countries there is also ample evidence of discrimination against such minorities, whether citizens, foreign workers or residents; and their unemployment rate tends to be significantly worse than for natives. In the Netherlands, for example, the share of foreign unemployment in total registered unemployment was 9.5 per cent in 1986, while the share of foreigners in the working population was much smaller, about 4.5 per cent. This disparity arises in part from the lower level of educational attainment among foreigners: the proportion with only primary education is for Dutch people 22 per cent, while for Turkish and Moroccan people the proportions are 74 and 84 per cent respectively. This disparity is also in part due to the relatively large proportion of older workers (age group 40–55 years) among the foreign population. However, even when the impact of differences in age and education is ignored, foreigners still have a lower chance to re-enter the labour market following a period of unemployment, probably for reasons of discrimination. Paradoxically, improvements in social rights for foreign workers have combined with labour market discrimination to create a new problem of welfare dependence. This is most notable in Germany, where the proportion of foreign households among those receiving regular social assistance has risen from 2.5 per cent in 1970 to 13.5 per cent, or 158 000 households, in 1985 and then further to 17.5 per cent in 1986 (Statistisches Bundesamt, 1970ff).

Women are a second vulnerable group. In the UK, government surveys of women and employment have confirmed that 'women work in a much more restricted number of occupations than men, with markedly fewer women in the very top jobs' (Martin and Roberts, 1985); that women are much more likely than men to be in less desirable occupations; and that they consistently earn a much lower hourly rate than men (Department of Employment, 1989). Across Europe, women are much more likely than men to be in part-time work (Table 6.6). As for unemployment, the difference between the male and female rates is especially striking in the case of

Table 6.6 Percentage of employees in part-time employment in EC countries

	% of total employees	*% of females*	*% of males*
Denmark	25.3	44.2	8.8
Netherlands	22.4	50.5	7.6
UK	21.7	44.5	4.0
West Germany	12.3	29.1	1.4
France	10.5	21.0	2.8
Belgium	9.3	23.2	1.8
Luxembourg	7.1	16.1	2.5
Ireland	5.8	12.7	2.1
Greece	4.4	8.3	2.6
Italy	4.5	8.6	2.4
All EC countries	13.3	29.1	3.0

Source: Hurstfield (1987), p. 4.

Table 6.7 Male and female unemployment rates (percentages)

	EUR 12	*B*	*DK*	*D*	*GR*	*E*	*F*	*IRL*	*I*	*L*	*NL*	*P*	*UK*
							Males and females						
1984	10.7	12.7	9.2	7.1	8.1	20.1	9.8	16.8	9.8	3.0	13.2	8.3	11.0
1985	10.9	11.9	8.2	7.4	7.8	21.9	10.3	18.3	9.2	3.1	10.5	8.6	11.6
1986	10.9	11.8	5.6	6.7	7.4	21.4	10.3	18.2	10.6	2.7	10.3	8.6	11.6
1987	10.7	11.6	5.9	6.6	7.4	21.2	10.7	19.4	10.6	3.1	10.0	7.1	10.9
							Males						
1984	9.4	8.7	8.1	6.2	6.0	19.0	7.8	16.3	6.6	2.3	11.8	5.5	11.5
1985	9.6	7.7	6.8	6.5	5.6	20.6	8.4	17.6	6.2	2.3	9.4	6.1	11.8
1986	9.4	7.5	4.0	5.6	5.1	19.7	8.6	17.5	7.1	2.0	8.9	6.8	11.9
1987	9.0	7.3	4.5	5.6	5.1	17.7	8.4	18.2	7.1	2.3	8.4	5.4	11.3
							Females						
1984	12.8	19.3	10.5	8.5	12.1	22.7	12.5	18.1	15.9	4.3	15.9	12.2	10.2
1985	13.0	18.7	9.8	8.9	11.7	25.1	12.8	19.7	14.9	4.6	12.7	12.1	11.1
1986	13.1	18.7	7.6	8.3	11.6	25.1	12.6	19.6	16.9	4.2	12.9	11.2	11.1
1987	13.4	18.5	7.5	8.1	11.5	28.5	13.6	22.1	17.1	4.6	13.0	9.4	10.3

NOTES:
This table shows the results of the Community labour force surveys carried out in spring 1983, 1984, 1985 and 1986 standardised for the month of April; the rates for April 1987 are estimated using the trends in national unemployment indicators.
Source: Eurostat (1988), p. 181.

Belgium, Greece, Italy and Portugal (Table 6.7).

The young also suffer higher than average confinement in part-time work and unemployment. Since the early 1980s they have figured prominently among the long-term unemployed (Rees, 1988, p. 6). As the OECD (1985) has pointed out, those born between the late 1950s and the mid-1960s have been particularly at risk of becoming long-term adult unemployed. Too old to enter training schemes for the young unemployed, they find it difficult to compete with better trained younger people (Rees, 1988, pp. 13–14). Despite the recent drop in the number of school-leavers joining the labour market, the young now constitute over a third of all unemployed people in the Community (Rees, 1988, p. 11). Thus in France in 1986, out of 8.5 million people aged 16–25, 2.8 million were students or still at school; and 3 million had a job in the strict sense of the term. Of the remainder, 1 million were unemployed and 650 000 were on various training courses and temporary job schemes.

For the young, the period before securing entry to the labour market is lengthening, 'making the transition from school to work a very difficult process' (Karantinos, 1987, p. 42). Indeed, high rates of youth unemployment and tighter restrictions upon entitlement to social assistance can impede the transition to adulthood and prolong childhood, by extending the period of dependence on parents (Rees, 1988, p. 6). Training programmes for the young, however much they may produce a more highly skilled labour force for the future, serve also to postpone adulthood (ibid., p. 19).

It is clear that many young people have become chronically dependent on social assistance and basic welfare. This reflects their confinement within, at most, the precarious section of the labour market, and their poor chances of building up any entitlement to unemployment insurance benefits. This is, to some extent, a feature of unemployment and poverty which distinguishes the 1970s and 1980s from previous periods of recession. Most governments have responded with more determined efforts to extend and improve educational training and work experience schemes. Despite such measures, however, significant numbers of young people remain more or less detached from either educational services or the labour market. It is their discouragement and despair that it is mainly responsible for the growing links revealed in recent research between unemployment, poverty, alcoholism, drugs and crime.

Evidence from many countries draws attention to the increasing problems, especially among the young, of homelessness or temporary care in hostels or low-grade 'bed and breakfast' accommodation (although there is very little reliable data on the changing size and composition of the homeless population). In Belgium, the work of the King Baudouin Foundation has revealed their extreme poverty. The composition of this population seems to have changed during recent years, with more people under 30 years of age, and many more young women, now being offered temporary shelter. Most of this group are single people; any employment they have had has been in the low wage and precarious sector; many have been involved with the penal authorities or the juvenile courts. Similar trends are evident in Germany, where the problem of *Nichtsesshaftigkeit* appears almost to have doubled between the early 1970s and mid-1980s, but with exceptionally large increases among younger age groups and women. Estimates of the numbers of homeless in the mid-1980s vary between one and two million people (including those in temporary homes); and of these, in a majority of cases unemployment appears to have been the predominant cause (Bolz, 1987, pp. 25–6).

On the margins of homelessness are those who, often as a result of unemployment and the rent arrears that frequently follow, find themselves relegated to the lowest quality tier of public housing, in a state of dilapidation far below normal social standards (Bolz, 1987, p. 25). Often physically separated from other neighbourhoods, such housing tends to consolidate their residents' separation from the information networks through which employment opportunities are frequently communicated; and from the networks of social support and social control by which communities which enjoy greater stability can withstand deprivation. And in countries such as Germany, such persons lack normal rights of tenancy and privacy, another deprivation of normal citizenship rights (Bolz, 1987, p. 26).

7 Poverty, the Family and the Life Cycle

Changes in the structure and the role of the family have had important effects on the distribution of poverty in the countries of the European Community. There have, moreover, been significant recent changes in the relationship between poverty and different phases of the life cycle.

This chapter argues, first, that the extent to which unemployment or an insecure position in the labour market leads to poverty depends crucially upon the family situation of the person concerned. Second, it examines the implications of the changes that have been taking place in family life styles: in particular, the rapid growth in the number of single parent families, who are at high risk of poverty in most Community countries. Finally, whereas poverty has been traditionally associated with large families and with specific phases of the life cycle, notably old age, the chapter considers how far this 'traditional' pattern has changed.

7.1 THE LABOUR MARKET, THE FAMILY AND POVERTY

The extent to which unemployment, or an insecure position in the labour market, leads to poverty depends crucially upon the person's family situation. If the family has other sources of employment income or, because of its composition, is entitled to additional state benefits, poverty may be avoided. Alternatively, however, the application of household means tests can mean that those who would otherwise be eligible to receive social assistance in their own right are forced instead to rely on their families. This is the case with many young people and women who, as seen in the previous chapter, are especially likely to lack entitlement to insurance benefits. Alongside growing dependence on 'last-resort' means-tested relief, therefore, is 'privatisation' of income support for the unemployed: twin processes which are evident in varying degrees throughout the European Community.

In France, for example, while recent policies have sought to improve the lot of older workers through early retirement and redundancy schemes, they have left many younger people and women primarily dependent during unemployment on support by their families. Hence, in France family solidarity has become the most critical factor influencing the financial circumstances of the long-term unemployed. This in turn renders more problematic the situation of those unemployed who cannot count on family solidarity of this sort, because they are single people or because they belong to a family where there is no other permanent income from work, retirement or social benefits. A similar picture, though with more stress on private and voluntary action, can be painted of the situation in Italy, Greece, Ireland and Portugal. All these countries have traditionally emphasised family solidarity as a primary source of 'social security', and their formal systems of unemployment benefits have been slower to develop than elsewhere in the EC.

In some countries, the rising costs of social assistance have made the public authorities more eager to enforce maintenance obligations on other members of the recipient's family. In Belgium, the local social assistance bureaux were formerly *permitted* to reclaim from responsible relatives payments of the Minimex benefit (the nationally guaranteed social assistance/supplementary benefit scheme which is administered at the local government level). Since 1984, however, they have been *required* to do so (Vandenbroucke, 1987, p. 16). This obligation has been criticised, for example by organisations concerned with the living conditions of families, on the one hand because of its deterrent effect *vis-à-vis* potential clients; and on the other hand because of the extra administrative costs which it imposes on the social assistance bureaux (ibid., p. 19; cf. Meulders-Klein and Eekelaar, 1988, vol. 1, pt 2).

Family solidarity can serve in other ways also to widen social inequalities. One distinctive feature of the present recession is the growing divide between families suffering multiple or total unemployment and the substantial numbers of 'working families' with more than one employed person. Although more information is needed on the factors underlying this, it is clearly related to the unequal incidence of unemployment, with its heavy concentration on poorer families, and in turn to the mechanisms by which the more powerful and organised in society have controlled access to employment. In those countries – such as Spain – where the female labour force participation ratio is low, there has been a greater risk of poverty for families having only one wage earner.

These inequalities have been exacerbated in the 1980s by the increase in means-testing for the unemployed, which create 'unemployment traps' which can discourage other family members from seeking work. It is important to stress, too, how the family dimensions of unemployment affect others, especially the elderly and disabled. The ability of families to care for their members, whether or not they are living together, is weakened when the standard of living of the younger members is reduced by unemployment.

7.2 ONE-PARENT FAMILIES AND POVERTY

The most widely publicised and controversial change in family life styles is the growing number of one-parent families, especially families headed by women. One-parent families now account for around 10 per cent of all families with children in France, Belgium, Germany and the Netherlands, and 14 per cent in the United Kingdom (Table 7.1). Moreover, a sharper rise is projected over the next quarter of a century: the British government, for example, estimates that by the year 2005 there will be 2.8 million one-parent families, compared with just over one million today (Family Policy Studies Centre, 1986, p. 2).

The increase in single parent families is one of the visible effects of changes in the family structure. While the increase is a long-term trend, it has accelerated in a number of EC countries since the late 1960s and early 1970s, a period which saw significant reforms in marriage and family law. Separation and divorce have become much more frequent in countries with previously restrictive legislation. In both Belgium and the Netherlands, for example, there was a threefold increase in divorce rates between the early 1970s and the mid-1980s. Even in Ireland, where the divorce law is at its most illiberal and the Catholic church retains much of its grip on family mores, the number of unmarried mothers receiving Unmarried Mothers Allowance nearly trebled between the mid-1970s and the mid-1980s. Elsewhere also, there have been increases in cohabitation and childbirth out of wedlock, which does not bear such a stigma as in the past, especially in urban areas. Widowhood, on the other hand, is of declining importance as a cause of single parenthood (O'Higgins, 1987, p. 8). Relatively few data are as yet available for the trends in the numbers of single parent families during the 1980s, but they indicate that the growth continues; and 'there is no evidence . . . of

Table 7.1 Single parent families as a percentage of all families with children, 1960–85

	1960	*1961*	*1968*	*1970*	*1971*	*1975*	*1976*	*1977*	*1980*	*1981*	*1982*	*1983*	*1984*	*1985*
Belgium	–	9.4	–	9.8	–	–	–	–	–	12.3	–	–	–	–
France	–	–	9.3	–	–	9.4	–	–	–	–	10.2	–	–	–
Germany	–	–	–	–	–	8.4	–	–	10.4	–	11.4	–		
Ireland	–	–	–	–	–	5.6	–	–	–	7.1	–	–	–	10.0
Netherlands	8.5	–	–	–	8.4	–	–	8.8	–	10.8	10.2	10.9	–	–
Spain	–	–	–	–	–	–	–	–	–	4.9	–	–	–	–
United Kingdom	–	–	–	–	8.0	–	10.0	–	–	–	–	–	13.0	–

Source: O'Higgins (1987), Table 2.

any peak or plateau now being reached' (O'Higgins, 1987, p. 7).

It is, of course, important not to exaggerate the extent or consequences of such trends for marriage and family life. The statistics refer to a given moment and represent fixed numbers, not 'flows'. Many single parent families are in a transitional situation, waiting to form or to reform a couple; and the evidence from France, for example, is that about half the situations of single parenthood have a duration of less than five years. Nevertheless, it is certain that a growing number of people have experienced or will experience the status of a single parent family; and the marked increase in such families includes many for whom single parenthood is more than a mere transitory phase.

The final report of the first European Programme to Combat Poverty identified one-parent families as a group with a particularly high risk of poverty, requiring priority attention in discussions of social security reform (Commission of the European Communities, 1981). In general, the circumstances of single parent families have worsened since the collection of data for that report. The main indication of this is their more widespread dependence on social assistance. Between the mid-1970s and mid-1980s, the number of one-parent families receiving means-tested assistance benefits rose in the United Kingdom, Germany, Belgium, the Netherlands and France (although in the French case at least, this increase resulted in part from the introduction in 1976 of the *Allocation de Parent Isolé*, a guaranteed minimum benefit for single parents with young children).

Poverty studies in the Netherlands and in the United Kingdom show that one-parent families experience far more poverty than other family types and in both countries there is substantial dependence on social assistance. Indeed, in 1985 over half of all one-parent families in the UK were receiving means-tested supplementary benefits (Table 5.5). In Germany, the number of households headed by single parents receiving regular aid from local social assistance rose from 105 000 in 1975 to 198 000 in 1985. The latter figure is still only 9 per cent of all one-parent households (rising to over 11 per cent one year later), but this is not necessarily a reflection of better 'first line' support than in other countries: it seems at least partly due to a more stringent code of relief applied to single parents. In Denmark, during the first quarter of 1982 three out of four single parents sought help from local welfare offices, because of illness, unemployment or increasing living costs: 40 per cent of all single mothers received regular social assistance and 50 per cent were below the EC poverty threshold. An even more disturbing trend was the growing numbers of single mothers on social assistance who were forced to place their children in local authority care: a 25 per cent increase was reported between 1978 and 1983.

The financial situation of single parent families depends, first, on the support provided by the former spouse (divorced and separated people) or life insurance policies which have been taken out by their deceased spouse (for widows). Hence the efforts of the public authorities to enforce maintenance obligations (Meulders-Klein and Eekelaar, 1988, vol. 1, pt 2). However, even if these obligations can be enforced, the resources which they provide are likely in many cases to be insufficient. This is because, although there are single parent families in all social classes, they are drawn disproportionately from those on modest incomes. This, in turn, is because people in this category are more likely to be exposed to the risks which create single parenthood: widowhood, divorce and childbirth out of wedlock.

The financial situation of single parent families depends, second, upon the employment opportunities which are available. These are obviously more limited for those who are poorly qualified or who have had to leave their work in order to bring up their children. Employment, moreover, often implies hours of work which need to be adapted to fit in with the needs of looking after children. Labour market participation by single parents varies greatly between countries: but in general, recent years show deteriorating trends. In Belgium, the UK and Spain the proportion of single mothers who work was, in the early 1980s at least, significantly less than half; and these proportions – in the UK and Belgium for example – are lower than in the late 1970s. Indeed, in the UK a smaller proportion of single mothers work part-time than mothers living with their husbands. This seems partly explained by poor or costly child care facilities, which offset the gains of part-time work for many one-parent families: hence their high dependence on Supplementary Benefit (Child Poverty Action Group, 1986/7, p. 19).

In Germany and France, in contrast, the rates of labour market participation for the same period were higher – at around 60 per cent and 75 per cent respectively. Nevertheless, in France the rate of unemployment for single parent families has been rising, from 10.8 per cent in 1982 to 14 per cent in 1985. In Denmark, which has long had a reputation for decent standards of support for single parent families, their access to the labour market has been greatly restricted by cuts in child care facilities and policies leading to disproportionately high female unemployment. In all of these countries, these deteriorating trends seem to reflect the impact of rising unemployment on these families' employment chances, coupled very often with cuts in child care provision as a result of public expenditure restrictions. However, it is also evident that the situation is changing rapidly and that we lack reliable information as to the situation in the late 1980s (O'Higgins, 1987, p. 25).

The financial circumstances of single parent families depend, finally, on the social benefits which are available to them. For the most part, single parents appear to have suffered from unfavourable changes in social protection. France, however, has been more vigorous in its efforts to meet their needs, notably by the introduction in 1976 of the *Allocation de Parent Isolé*, a guaranteed minimum benefit for single parents with young children. API is given on the basis of existing resources and represents the differential allowance between family resources and a ceiling which varies according to the size of the family (in 1986 2525Fr for a pregnant woman, 3367Fr for a parent with one child, 841Fr per additional child).

However, these attempts to provide alternative compensatory and selective social provisions have been surrounded by controversy. Since the introduction of API, some have seen in it the risk of encouraging unmarried motherhood or the concealment of informal unions as a result of the higher level of benefit which it offers; and more generally the danger of promoting a 'mentality of assistance', along with a disincentive to seek work. Recent studies do not, however, confirm this phenomenon of discouragement: it is the unemployment situation that makes it difficult to find work. In addition, although the number of people receiving API greatly increased in the early 1980s, i.e. beyond the increase of the allowance, it now seems to be levelling out. Nevertheless, such controversy helps to explain why this benefit has remained restricted in duration to 12 months, or until the youngest child has reached the age of three, which in turn has led to a critical financial situation among those who have exhausted their rights to API. Hence, as with the unemployed, such *ad hoc* and selective measures have had only a limited impact in reducing hardship and poverty. Nevertheless, it is clear that 'lone parenthood is now an integral part of the fabric of social experience in most European countries; public policies must be designed to integrate that experience with common employment, mobility and income levels rather than isolate it in dependent poverty' (O'Higgins, 1987, p. 43).

7.3 CHILDREN AND POVERTY

Recent economic and social trends mean that poverty now mostly affects children and adults of working age. O'Higgins and Jenkins (1989) refer, for the period between 1975 and 1985, to a 'variety of . . . evidence in these countries indicating a shift towards families with children in the distribution of poverty'. In Italy, for example, 40 per cent of the poor were found in 1983 to be found in the central age brackets (ages 25–65); 18.3 per cent to fall between ages 14 and 25; and 20.4 per cent to be younger than 14 years old (Italian Commission on Poverty, 1985). In Ireland, in the period from 1973 and 1980, households with children became markedly more significant among the ranks of the poor, especially the very poor (Nolan, 1987, 1989); and during the 1980s, this development has accelerated (Combat Poverty Agency, 1988).

However, with the partial exception of Ireland, where fertility has been much higher than in other EC countries, the ranks of poor families are no longer constituted mainly by larger families (see also Section 5.3 above). This is partly because of the growing significance of single parenthood as a factor associated with family poverty: for, as O'Higgins shows, substantial proportions of children are now living in single parent families (O'Higgins, 1987, p. 20). However, this is not the only factor leading to a spreading or re-distribution of the risk of family poverty. Italy is of particular interest, because of the contrast between the traditional poverty of the South and its newer dimensions in the Centre-North regions of the country. In the South, a high percentage of the poor (46 per cent according to the Italian Commission on Poverty of 1985) live in families with five or more members, but in the Centre-North the proportion is only one-quarter of the poor. More significantly, the highest concentration of poverty in the Centre-North is now found in the 'typical' four-person family: 539 564 individuals out of the Centre-North's total of 2.5 million poor (Italian Commission on Poverty, 1985). Even in the south of Italy, as in the other more rural countries of the Mediterranean, the percentage of the poor who belong to large families seems to be declining.

This suggests that a new dimension of poverty may be the vulnerability of children in smaller families. In Italy, for example, 20 per cent of the poor in the mid-1980s were younger than 14 years old; and some 460 000 children below age five were living in poverty (Italian Commission on Poverty, 1985). Unfortunately, however, most national statistics on poverty or social assistance provide little insight into this, and where data exist, the evidence is conflicting. The Belgian surveys by the Centre for Social Policy in Antwerp suggest, for example, an increase in the risk of poverty or 'insecurity or subsistence' among families with one or two children between 1976 and 1982, and at the same time a marked drop in poverty amongst households with three or more children. Between 1982 and 1985, however, all families with children show a reduced risk of poverty. British official estimates of the changing low income population reveal a different picture. In 1983, 16 per cent of all children, or over two million, were living in families with incomes on or below Supplementary Benefit levels, a 72 per cent increase since 1979. Nearly four million children, almost one third of all children in Great Britain, were in families living in poverty or on the margins of poverty (meaning by this incomes below 140 per cent of Supplementary Benefit levels): of these, 1.3 million were in families of the unemployed, 1.4 million in the families of low paid workers and over 900 000 in one-parent families (Child Poverty Action Group, 1986/7).

As for young people, the previous chapter noted how high rates of unemployment and restrictions on individual rights to social benefits can force a prolonged period of dependence on parents and impede the transition to adulthood. These barriers are reinforced elsewhere in the welfare system also. In Spain, for example, health care coverage of unemployed young people has been secured not by providing them with rights themselves, but rather by extending the age limit for 'dependent children' to 26 years (Duran and Lopez-Arribas, 1987, p. 14). Some commentators see teenage pregnancy as being, in part, an alternative strategy for achieving the transition to adult status, even if childcare responsibilities then make it still more difficult for single parents in particular to enter the labour market (Rees, 1988, pp. 6, 19).

7.4 THE ELDERLY

There has, it is clear, been a marked shift in the composition of the poor away from elderly towards younger households (see Section 5.3). This is a consequence not only of the growing risks of poverty among younger families and single persons but also of more effective national pensions and welfare policies for the elderly. The living standards of old people have generally improved, as a result of the maturing of state and occupational pension rights; and minimum income guarantees and housing and welfare benefits have given the elderly better protection against inflation than groups such as the unemployed or single parents.

Thus, for example, in Germany there is ample evidence of a significant absolute and relative fall in the risk of poverty among old people since around 1975. The Italian Poverty Commission noted for 1983 that 'from the qualitative point of view, poverty among the elderly has specific traits of its own and generally entails a high level of distress. None the less, the statistics indicate that although the probability of poverty is higher among the elderly than in the population at large, the phenomenon of poverty among the elderly – measured only in terms of a serious shortfall of income – affects fewer individuals than is commonly believed' (Italian Commission on Poverty, 1985).

In France, pensioners whose contributory pension is insufficient receive a means-tested addition from the Fonds National de Solidarité (FNS). The resulting guaranteed minimum pension (*minimum vieillesse*) has had its real value increased considerably, rising by a factor of 2.5 between 1970 and the mid-1980s, due to an active policy of revaluation. At the same time, the number of those who benefit from the FNS has steadily decreased, as seen in Table 5.1, due to the better cover afforded to the elderly by the social security system and normal pension schemes.

On closer inspection, however, important qualifications need to be made to this picture. In a number of EC countries, old people, while constituting a smaller proportion of the poor than in the past, are still substantially at risk of poverty. In Italy, for example, although the vast majority of the elderly population now enjoys a level of consumer spending above the threshold of poverty, it nevertheless remains the case that in 1983 1 360 000 persons aged 65 and over were classified as being poor. Likewise, in the United Kingdom, where the number of pensioners claiming means-tested supplementary benefits has fallen slightly, elderly people remain by far the largest group living below the 'official' poverty line, often alone, often in owner-occupied houses in bad repair, and frequently without the kind of local authority domiciliary support which would make independent living a good option. The incidence of inadequate nutrition and heating which local authority and other studies have found among the elderly leaves no room for complacency.

It is also clear that the poorer EC countries have faced more formidable problems in improving pensions and other benefits. In Portugal, for example, since 1973 the average value of the old age and invalidity pension of the contributory scheme has remained below the poverty line for one adult-equivalent living in urban centres, with an increasing gap after 1976. In Greece, although the incidence of poverty among the elderly population has been falling, the elderly have (at least during the period until 1981/82) formed a growing proportion of the poor population (Tables 5.2, 5.4).

There are also signs that the general improvement of living standards among the elderly hides widening disparities of incomes and welfare in the older population. It is therefore necessary to emphasise the great variety of situations which retirement includes, where one finds many of the inequalities of working life reproduced. Perhaps more significant, however, are the disparities associated with the considerable shift which has been occurring recently in the age structure of the elderly population and which will become even more pronounced over the next 20 years or so. As a number of recent studies have emphasised, the emergence of a 'new class of the very old' is of immense significance for poverty and social policy. It is already resulting in increasing numbers of old people living alone or in poor health because of their advanced age. It is also revealing in stark terms the shortcomings of existing policies, particularly those arrangements under which men have traditionally gained higher pensions and benefits than women and greater access to resources generally (see, for example, Walker et al., 1984).

At the same time, the challenge of meeting these new needs is greatly complicated by another, and on the face of it paradoxical, development. At a time when the very old are growing in numbers, there has also been a growth in early retirement (mainly as a result of unemployment) and a dramatic decline in the proportions of the 'young old' who are in employment (Table 6.2). In Denmark, for example, the 1970s and 1980s have seen vigorous government efforts to develop early retirement schemes, as a means of dealing with unemployment. Early retirement is often justified in terms of disability, because of the higher rates of pension that this involves (Abrahamson et al., 1987, pp. 20–1). In France, the numbers taking early retirement increased from 76 800 in 1975 to 215 500 in 1980 and then to 660 000 in 1984. Early retirement schemes can of course improve the lot of many older people. Nevertheless, the incomes of the early retired are often relatively low (albeit better than the unemployed), since early retirement schemes are often dependent on wages and work records which, for those retiring prematurely, are often poor.

Most serious of all, however, is the prospect for today's long-term unemployed when they eventually retire. Their interrupted work and contribution records are likely to mean that the unemployment which separated them from the bulk of the working population during their working lives will turn them into a new class of the elderly poor during the coming decades. In the Netherlands, for example, there has been growing concern over the question of 'frozen pensions': the loss of pension rights which occurs as a result of unemployment and job changes.

Finally, of course, the rising costs of pensions, as a result of an

Table 7.2 Proportion of population aged 65 or over, 1960–2040 (per cent)

			Projections		
	1960	*1986*	*2000*	*2020*	*2040*
Australia	8.5	10.5	11.7	15.5	20.0
Austria	11.9	14.5	14.9	19.4	24.4
Belgium	12.0	14.1	15.0	18.5	22.3
Canada	7.6	10.7	12.9	18.8	22.7
Denmark	n.a.	15.3	14.9	20.1	25.2
Finland	7.5	12.7	14.6	21.7	23.2
France	11.6	13.2	15.2	19.5	23.1
Germany	10.6	15.1	17.0	21.7	28.0
Greece	8.1	13.0	15.0	17.9	21.2
Iceland	8.1	10.1	10.9	14.4	20.3
Ireland	11.1	10.9	11.2	12.7	17.2
Italy	9.1	13.1	15.4	19.1	24.9
Japan	5.7	10.5	15.1	21.0	22.7
Luxembourg	n.a.	13.4	16.8	20.3	22.3
Netherlands	8.6	12.3	13.5	19.0	25.0
New Zealand	8.6	10.5	11.1	15.2	21.9
Norway	11.1	16.0	15.0	18.2	23.1
Portugal	n.a.	12.2	13.3	15.4	20.6
Spain	n.a.	12.8	14.6	17.9	23.3
Sweden	11.8	17.5	16.6	20.8	22.8
Switzerland	11.0	14.7	16.8	24.4	28.6
Turkey	n.a.	4.1	5.1	6.9	10.5
United Kingdom	11.7	15.3	14.5	16.4	20.6
United States	9.2	12.1	12.2	16.2	20.0
OECD average	9.7	12.7	13.9	18.0	22.2

Source: OECD (1988a), Table 4.

Table 7.3 Proportion of population aged 75 or over, 1960–2040 (percent)

				Projections	
	1960	*1986*	*2000*	*2020*	*2040*
Australia	2.7	4.0	5.1	6.2	9.8
Austria	4.0	6.8	6.5	8.9	12.3
Belgium	4.2	6.4	5.9	7.3	10.6
Canada	2.7	4.1	5.5	7.6	12.0
Denmark	n.a.	6.5	6.7	8.0	11.4
Finland	2.4	5.2	6.2	8.5	12.1
France	4.3	6.4	6.5	8.2	11.7
Germany	3.4	7.0	7.1	9.8	14.1
Greece	3.0	5.4	4.8	7.5	9.1
Iceland	2.9	4.3	4.4	5.0	9.1
Ireland	4.2	4.0	5.3	4.8	7.0
Italy	3.0	5.7	6.0	8.1	10.9
Japan	1.8	4.0	5.4	8.3	9.8
Luxembourg	n.a.	6.0	7.0	8.9	11.6
Netherlands	2.8	5.1	5.8	7.1	12.2
New Zealand	3.2	4.1	4.7	5.6	9.7
Norway	4.0	6.6	7.5	7.1	10.9
Portugal	n.a.	4.8	5.0	6.3	8.6
Spain	n.a.	5.0	5.8	7.5	10.4
Sweden	4.1	7.5	8.1	9.0	10.9
Switzerland	3.5	6.8	7.5	11.7	15.8
Turkey	n.a.	1.5	1.2	2.0	3.2
United Kingdom	4.2	6.5	6.3	6.5	9.9
United States	3.1	5.0	5.5	6.0	10.2
OECD average	3.3	5.4	5.8	7.3	10.6

Source: OECD (1988a), Table 5.

ageing population (Tables 7.2, 7.3) – and the burden that this imposes on the population of working age – mean that it would be wrong to assume that poverty among the aged has now been 'solved'. In the Netherlands, for example, demographic changes will mean that the costs of the General Old Age Scheme (AOW) will be twice as high in 2030 as in 1982 (Nelissen and Vossen, 1984). This demographic shift does not affect only pensions. In Germany, for example, the costs for a place in a nursing home have been rising faster than pensions. Occupants of these homes are therefore becoming increasingly reliant on social assistance benefits. Either this will continue, or else an increasing proportion of the costs will be shifted onto the elderly themselves and their relatives: again, a 'privatisation' of income support (Bolz, 1987, p. 24).

7.5 THE 'FEMINISATION' OF POVERTY?

To what extent do the trends which have been traced in the preceding pages involve the 'feminisation' of poverty?

First, as seen in Section 6.4, women have in general continued to occupy the less advantaged positions within the workforce, with less security, lower pay and poorer levels of social protection. Their labour force participation is increasing, and thus their opportunity to earn their own rights to social protection; however, this increased participation is concentrated in the 'secondary' labour market (Section 6.3), with its inferior forms of social protection. Not surprisingly, therefore, women continue to be heavily over-represented among those who depend on social assistance-type supplements to pensions and other benefits. In Spain, for example, it is women who are predominant among the approximately 330 000 beneficiaries of social assistance pensions (financed and regulated nationally but administered at regional level), because they are more likely to have a poor employment record. Those – predominantly men – who have a better employment record, but lack an adequate pension, are able to receive various supplements within the social security scheme which, although income tested, are not seen as part of the social assistance scheme.

There are some trends in the opposite direction. In Ireland, the incidence of poverty among female-headed households has greatly fallen, relative to the incidence among male-headed households (Combat Poverty Agency, 1988, p. 44). In Belgium and Germany, similarly, the period since the mid-1970s has seen substantial falls in the proportion of social assistance recipients who are women. Nevertheless, in all these cases these improvements appear to be age-related: the result, in other words, of the improved protection against poverty which is enjoyed by elderly people, the majority of whom are women. Among younger people, female-headed households continue to suffer higher rates of poverty than male-headed ones (Combat Poverty Agency, 1988, p. 44).

It is, however, the growth in the numbers of single parent families that is perhaps the most often cited aspect of the 'feminisation' of poverty. The heads of single parent families are, to an increasing extent, female. This is, in large measure, because widowhood is declining as a cause of single headedness. Not only is single parenthood increasing, therefore; it is also increasingly characterised by female headedness, 'with women receiving a higher proportion of the primary child care responsibilities' (O'Higgins, 1987, p. 11).

Finally, the growing numbers of elderly people – especially the very old – and the attempts by many governments, to shift the burden of care from public institutions back to the family, are likely to impinge in particular upon women, the traditional carers for the young and the old. Much broader questions are therefore raised concerning the traditional division of labour between men and women in regards to the care of the dependent: a division which plays a major part in ensuring that women are more likely than men to experience poverty.

8 Poverty North and South

8.1 INTRODUCTION

The 1980s have seen the European Community expanding to include the southern countries of Greece, Spain and Portugal. In consequence, the Community and its institutions have been obliged to address themselves to the problems of structural underdevelopment on an altogether greater scale than when such problems were largely confined to Ireland and southern Italy. Central to the Community's efforts to prepare for the advent of the Single Market in 1992 is an expansion and reorganisation of its structural funds, in order to promote training and infrastructure investment in the structurally backward regions of the south.

In this study of poverty in the European Community, it is, similarly, essential to consider the distinctive patterns of poverty which are associated with the long-standing social and economic underdevelopment of these countries, even though for some of them, reliable data are scarce, as was evident in the tables presented in Chapter 5. These countries have long been poor. During recent years, however, major changes have been taking place within them. This is partly the result of their being incorporated into the European Community; but it is also because, like their new partners, they have been exposed to major changes in the international economy.

Table 8.1 Sectoral shares in total employment, 1970–86 (percentages)

	Agriculture		*Industry*		*Services*	
	1970	*1986*	*1970*	*1986*	*1970*	*1986*
Greece	38.8	27.2	23.8	26.8	37.4	46.0
Ireland	26.9	15.6	29.6	28.0	43.5	56.4
Spain	28.5	15.6	36.0	31.0	35.5	53.4
	1975	*1986*	*1975*	*1986*	*1975*	*1986*
Portugal	32.8	21.5	32.7	33.5	34.5	45.0

Source: Commission of the European Communities (1988d), table A11.

One obvious transformation has been the large-scale transfer of population out of agriculture, as is typical of economic modernisation (Table 8.1). In Greece, as an accompaniment of general economic growth, the last 30 years have seen a large-scale 'transfer of surplus labour from the rural areas to the urban centres', raising the per capita incomes of the remaining rural population and often enhancing this through remittances from the migrants. During the three post-war decades the population of Athens, for example, more than doubled (Karantinos, 1987, p. 5). Disparities of income between urban and rural areas have remained high, providing a continuing inducement to further internal migration (ibid., pp. 5–6). There has also been a strong 'development of services and industry at the expense of agricultural activities' (ibid., pp. 4, 6). These changes have had a strong impact on the distribution of the poor population of these countries. In Portugal, for example, whereas in the previous generation a quarter of the heads of low income households were agricultural employees, today the figure has fallen to a mere tenth. In contrast, the proportion who are non-agricultural employees has risen from 30 per cent to almost 45 per cent (da Costa et al., 1985).

A second transformation has involved the introduction of new measures of social protection and education programmes, in imitation of the northern neighbours. In Greece, for example, since the 1970s the government has sought to fill the gaps in existing social insurance provisions (Karantinos, 1987, p. 21); and at an institutional level, to improve the coordination of the activities of the large range of public and private agencies working in the welfare field (ibid, p. 22). The overall result of these economic changes and advances in social protection has been a dramatic fall in the extent of absolute poverty, which has disappeared as a mass phenomenon (ibid., pp. 2–3).

In Spain, similarly, a rapid increase in social security contributions during the 1970s furnished expanded resources for health service and income maintenance programmes. 'Despite its shortcomings, the social welfare system has consolidated its position over the last decade, extending health care to nearly everybody, and old age and invalidity pensions to the great majority' (Duran and Lopez-Arribas, 1987, pp. 12, 16). In Ireland (which for the purpose of the present chapter can to some extent be included among the countries of the 'south'), reforms in the system of income maintenance during the 1970s – and in particular the raising of benefit levels – 'led to a significant reduction of poverty' (Roche, 1984, p. 153). This was accompanied by a progressive redistribution of income and, in Dublin at least, significant improvements in the availability of public housing, including housing for single parents and unmarried mothers.

As in the northern and richer countries of Europe, therefore, poverty is increasingly an urban phenomenon and one that is linked to activities in the secondary and tertiary sectors (even if, at least in Greece, the risk of poverty is higher for the rural population than for the urban: Karantinos, 1987, p. 12). In Portugal, for example, more than half the heads of low income households are concentrated outside agriculture. Not surprisingly, some of the newly emergent aspects of poverty which these countries display resemble those in the more affluent European nations whose economic and social development they are taking as their model. In Portugal, for example, precarious employment has developed on a wide scale, involving delays by employers in the payment of wages; and there was a significant decline in the real value of the minimum wage, from its institution in 1974 until the early 1980s, so that it failed to protect the employed against poverty. In Greece, as in the north, an increasing proportion of the unemployed have been long-term unemployed (up from 2.9 per cent in 1974 to 37.1 per cent in 1984: see Table 6.4) and during the 1980s the proportion of the unemployed who are made up of the young has remained close to the Community average. Earlier chapters of this report have pointed to many other respects in which these southern countries have been struggling to cope with the same challenges and dilemmas as their richer neighbours.

Nevertheless, the contrasts between north and south in the scale and form of poverty remain very considerable. In Italy, for example, the risk of poverty remains more than twice as high in the south as in the centre and north of the country; and 70 per cent of poor children (less than 14 years) are living in the south (Italian Commission on Poverty, 1985). Similarly, in the south of Italy, registered unemployment runs at twice the level for the north of the country: and to this must be added the underemployment of structurally underdeveloped rural areas.

There are a number of reasons for this persistence of high rates of poverty in the south. First, while the structural changes already mentioned have clearly reduced the extent of absolute poverty, concentrated within the rural areas, there is some evidence that in the urban areas, for example in Greece, there is 'increased economic inequality and hence relative poverty' (Karantinos, 1987, p. 4). During the 1970s, the large-scale influx of migrants from rural areas 'led to the disruption of the urban labour markets' (ibid., p. 7); the jobs available were in general unskilled, insecure and low paid (ibid., p. 7); and low levels of unemployment protection have meant that few could afford to refuse such jobs for any extended period of time (ibid., p. 7). Since the mid-1970s, however, 'much of the disequilibrium in the urban labour markets caused by internal migration appears to have been absorbed' (ibid., p. 7).

Second, after a period of convergence among the regions of the Community during the 1960s and 1970s, due to faster growth in the poorer regions and inter-regional migration, there seems to have been a reversal in more recent years (Commission of the European Communities, 1987). More rapid population growth in the underdeveloped regions and reduced opportunities for migration to the more advanced regions are likely to reinforce this divergence. Even within the countries of the South, population transfer to the more advanced regions has slowed during the 1980s. In Portugal, for example, high levels of urban unemployment have deterred continuing migration from the rural areas (da Costa, 1986, p. 10). In Spain, similarly, massive migration off the land during the 1960s and 1970s 'allowed an increase in the land available per worker and thus improved productivity and reduced poverty'. In the 1980s, however, migration has become more difficult. As a result, 'the problem of land reform is again a pressing one in those areas in which rural unemployment is high and in which there are estates of great size and non-intensive agricultural methods'. Two of the autonomous regions have launched programmes of land reform, but have encountered legal problems in carrying them out. Nevertheless, they continue to come under pressure from potential beneficiaries, who in some cases are resorting to direct squatting on the land (Duran and Lopez-Arribas, 1987, p. 13).

Third, it is clear that the international recession, and the associated austerity and inflation, have severely limited the expansion of social benefits in these countries, or even the maintenance of social benefits at their previous levels. Thus in 1987, in Italy, Portugal and Greece, total expenditure on unemployment compensation fell below 0.5 per cent of GDP, the only Community countries apart from Luxembourg, with its much lower rate of unemployment, to do so (OECD, 1988b, table 3.1). In August 1983, only 11 per cent of the unemployed in Portugal were receiving unemployment subsidy. As to the level of benefit, this varied with the number of dependants, but only when the latter numbered six or more did the unemployment benefit reach the level of the national minimum wage. More generally, a range of social security benefits in Portugal are geared to the level of the minimum wage, but the real value of the latter appears to have been falling steadily (da Costa, 1987, p. 2).

To some extent, new poverty problems in these countries reflect the pace of social changes brought about by modernisation programmes and the distortions and difficulties for these programmes resulting from recent adverse economic trends. Ireland, during a period of rapid economic growth following entry into the EC, sought to modernise rapidly its social security and welfare provisions; but it has found it increasingly difficult to reconcile these commitments with the harsher economic climate of the 1980s. In Greece, programmes of modernisation have both encouraged and provide more social protection for the rapidly increasing numbers of smaller families, but at the same time have placed the traditional multi-member family at a disadvantage. In Greece, Spain and Portugal, the rapid expansion of higher education has combined with the economic crisis to produce increasing numbers of university graduates who are not easily absorbed into the labour market. This has a – less academic – counterpart in the new 'middle-class' unemployment which during the mid-1980s was much discussed in Ireland, as being one of the most obvious manifestations of 'new poverty' in that country.

The recent poverty problems of the southern countries have also been exacerbated by the policy choices made by the more prosperous member states. This is particularly evident in relation to migration. The 1960s and early 1970s saw large-scale migration from southern to northern Europe: for example, between 1960 and 1974 around 690 000 Greek workers (including their families) migrated to northern Europe in search of employment. The majority, 609 000, went to West Germany. The end of recruitment of migrant workers in the mid-1970s meant a large-scale return to the southern countries of origin. For example, of the Greek population in Germany, 309 000 returned to Greece between 1974 and 1980. Many have found it difficult to re-establish themselves in Greek society and they have suffered from the severe lack of appropriate counselling services in both Germany and Greece. Repatriation to Greece of political refugees from eastern Europe and to Portugal of former colonial residents has added to these problems.

As in northern Europe, the relationship between unemployment and poverty depends on entitlement to social security on the one hand and family solidarity on the other. As noted above, however, the social security systems in some of these countries are not well developed; the family is an alternative – and older – system of 'social security'. Those sections of the population who, as a result of rapid programmes of modernisation and urbanisation, lose the security of the traditional family structure, are likely to find themselves particularly vulnerable as unemployment levels rise. In Portugal, for example, between 1973/4 and 1980 the percentage of poor households consisting of single persons doubled (da Costa et al., 1985). Acute processes of marginalisation were evident in southern Italy, in particular during the 1970s, as the industrialisation of the south led to the hypertrophy of several urban areas, often taking the form of a clash between the industrial world and the peasant world which penetrated even the family. Similarly, urbanisation has produced changes in the Greek family which reduce intergenerational interdependence; and the increasing concentration of unemployment into urban areas – even though the official data may undertake the extent of unemployment and underemployment in rural areas (Karantinos, 1987, p. 41) – suggests that many of these unemployed may now lack the security of the traditional family structure. Meanwhile, with 'the ageing of the population proceeding faster in the rural areas', the 'immense human cost of migration' affects all age groups and both rural and urban areas (Karantinos, 1987, pp. 4, 32).

It remains to be seen how far the attempt at accelerated modernisation of their agricultural, industrial and communications infrastructure, through the operation of the expanded structural funds of the European Community, will contribute effectively to these economic and social insecurities. The signs are not all favourable. In Ireland, for example, critics have pointed to the uneven development of farms under the impact of the Common Agricultural Policy, and the further marginalisation of the smaller, low productivity farms in the more remote areas (Kelleher, 1987, p. 5).

While, therefore, it is difficult in these countries of the South to record the arithmetic of poverty with the detail of their northern neighbours, it is clear that these societies are confronting forms of poverty which deserve more intensive examination.

9 Government Responsibility and Response

9.1 DIVISIONS OF WELFARE

Previous chapters have highlighted new dimensions of poverty in the 1970s and 1980s. However, it is important to recognise the extent to which the 'new poverty' is rooted in older problems and developments that occurred prior to the 1970s. Many of the issues discussed here are related to the absence in most member states of effective 'citizenship' rights to a decent minimum standard of living. As the European Commission's final report of the first Programme to Combat Poverty emphasised, the gaps in the European welfare states have remained 'large and cavernous' throughout the post-war period (Commission of the European Communities, 1981). This is primarily because the most elaborate and costly forms of social protection have favoured workers with regular and stable employment. In practice, they have benefited a wide middle stratum of society, while neglecting many others and leaving them poorly protected, relying mainly on national or local social assistance measures.

During the period of full employment, this latter group consisted mostly of immigrant workers and women (who especially in old age suffered from poor protection), various low-paid, poorly qualified and marginal workers, and, in some member states, certain self-employed persons and workers in agriculture and retail trades. As we have seen, however, their ranks have been swelled dramatically over the past decade, particularly with the erosion of social insurance protection, as a result of high rates of unemployment and the growth of precarious employment.

The policies pursued by a number of European governments have tended to accentuate disparities in social protection. In Denmark, for example, following the election of a conservative government in 1982, the social assistance system was standardised and simplified, but with many long-term recipients, in particular, suffering a reduced level of benefit (Abrahamson et al., 1987, pp. 18–19). In Germany, those who are dependent for their livelihood on local social assistance were more severely hit by the cuts and retrenchment between the late 1970s and mid-1980s than were most social insurance beneficiaries. During this period, basic rates of social assistance fell significantly behind levels of inflation and the code of relief was toughened, partly because of the pressures put on regional and local government finances by the declining effectiveness of national social and labour policies. At the same time, dependence on assistance was increased, as a result of cuts in labour market programmes and a lengthening of contribution requirements for unemployment insurance. By contrast, despite cuts in social insurance provisions, those with relative security of employment continued to enjoy relatively high standards of social security, as well as preserving their relative position in the income hierarchy.

In Belgium, those in the lower income brackets may not have suffered in absolute terms as a result of the cuts in social benefits. One of the policy priorities in each of the official government platforms of 1981, 1984 and 1985 was 'priority to the deprived'. During the whole period of retrenchment policies from 1982 onwards, minimum benefit levels were adapted in line with the consumer price index. However, low income households suffered higher rates of inflation than the population in general, which were not necessarily entirely offset by the inflation proofing mechanism. *Ad hoc* increases in selective minimum benefit levels did not, therefore, necessarily represent real increases in purchasing power. Overall, it remains doubtful whether the government achieved its objective of protecting in real terms the position of the most disadvantaged groups of the population (de Boeck, 1987).

In the Netherlands, means-tested benefits are becoming more significant, under reforms of the social security system introduced in 1987. The predictable result is an increasingly serious 'poverty trap', especially for incomes just above the social minimum (Muffels and de Vries, 1987, pp. 30–1). In the UK, the growth in the numbers of people who are dependent on means-tested assistance produced increasing strain and confusion within the social security system, which became the subject of a major review and new legislation (Social Security Act, 1986). Detailed provisions under the new Act have been coming into force progressively since July 1986. A controversial feature of the Act was the introduction of a new Social Fund, replacing payments for special needs under the Supplementary Benefits scheme with new discretionary payments, mainly in the form of loans to the poor. This has aroused considerable fears that the latter will suffer as a result of the changes.

However, it is not only in the field of social security that more restrictive policies have had some ill effects on the less advantaged groups in society. In many countries, the growing numbers of homeless bear witness not only to the effects of unemployment upon people's capacity to buy or rent housing, but also to a diminution in the supply of housing which is within the reach of lower income groups. In the UK, for example, the last decade has seen a sharp decrease in the construction of new public housing, as result of expenditure restrictions imposed by central government; and, as a result of the purchase of local authority dwellings by their tenants, under the legislation of the Conservative goverment, there has been a substantial reduction in the stock of housing available to local authorities for meeting urgent housing needs.

9.2 GOVERNMENT RESPONSES TO THE NEW POVERTY

Emergency Relief

Some recent measures have been concerned with the more visible manifestations of poverty. During the mid-1980s, the French government's programmes specifically in relation to poverty concentrated upon emergency accommodation, food aid, rent and fuel debts, etc. Similarly, the European Community itself has been involved in programmes of 'Winter Aid', involving the distribution of food surpluses to the needy. These programmes have, however, drawn an often critical response from many of the welfare agencies which have been involved and which see them as a reversion to an archaic and paternalistic form of charity.

Changes in the composition of the homeless population have encouraged the development, in Belgium for example, of hostels to care for the female homeless, care centres for young people and so-called half-way houses. However, punitive measures have also grown in frequency: and in Belgium, between 1963 and 1982, the number of internments based on the law against vagabondage increased from 1283 to 2246.

New Directions in Social Protection

Many governments have made considerable efforts to combine austerity programmes with safeguards for the poorest in society, though with varying degrees of success. One strategy has been to relax the conditions of eligibility for unemployment benefit. In Greece, new entrants to the labour force have since 1985 been entitled to unemployment benefits if they do not find a job within six months of their initial registration (Karantinos, 1987, p. 45). In Germany, since the beginning of 1986, older unemployed persons (over 50) have been able to receive unemployment compensation for two years, not one.

Another strategy has been to develop non-contributory unemployment assistance alongside unemployment benefit proper. Thus in 1985, Portugal introduced a non-contributory social subsidy for unemployment, for workers who have exhausted their entitlement to unemployment benefit. In Spain, the establishment of pension minima and income-related 'supplements' has changed the purely contributory character of the social security system; but these new elements have been kept separate from social assistance as such and the administration of the latter has increasingly been devolved to regional and local government (Duran and Lopez-Arribas, 1987). The Spanish government has promised a non-contributory pension law.

A third strategy has been to reform the systems of local social assistance, the traditional last resort of the needy. During the mid-1980s, France adopted a series of anti-poverty measures aimed particularly at ameliorating the conditions of those who had exhausted their rights to national benefits, by improving and coordinating local and voluntary social action. However, such measures in turn served to focus attention on the limitations and difficulties of an emphasis on local administration and social work in combatting poverty. Variations between the services provided by different *departements* and communes, problems of financing and the emergency character of many of the measures became a matter of growing concern. More fundamentally, they served to re-open the debate about national solidarity and the authority of the state in relation to the poor, and more specifically the debates about the insufficiency of existing *national* guaranteed income measures. The present social government has therefore launched a new scheme of guaranteed minimum income (*revenu minimum d'insertion*).

Similar pressures for a thorough re-appraisal and reform of the national 'social minima' are evident in some other member states, such as Belgium and the Netherlands. In both countries these have arisen out of government efforts, only partially successful, to give priority to the 'truly deprived' (*echta minima*). During the period of severe retrenchment in the first half of the 1980s, increases in basic minimum benefits, especially for families reliant on one source of income, exceeded those of wages and other social security benefits. However, because of high inflation rates among low income families it is doubtful whether many minimum income beneficiaries improved their position in real terms.

Luxembourg, the other Benelux country, has also made vigorous efforts to develop a minimum guaranteed income. The Law of July 1986, creating the right to such a guaranteed minimum, derived from a report of the Economic and Social Council of Luxembourg, which itself took as a point of reference the Schaber poverty studies in Luxembourg, sponsored in part by the EC during the period 1975–80. This minimum income is intended, in general, to be reserved for those who are available for, and seeking, work; and it is linked to efforts to lead beneficiaries progressively into the labour market, via retraining, etc.

Many of these initiatives have meant changes in the division of financial and administrative responsibility for income support between central government and local or regional government. And some of them, of course, have been instigated as a result of pressure from these 'lower' levels of government, as they faced the rising tide of demands for assistance, with the systems of traditional relief proving inadequate or costly. Thus, for example, in France, local initiatives in providing a minimum income (CERC, 1988) supplied the stimulus for the larger national effort initiated by the socialist government in 1988. In Spain, similarly, the Basque Regional Law which establishes a minimum wage similar to the French *revenue minimum d'insertion* is stimulating other autonomous communities and the central government. Rather differently, in the UK, with its national system of social assistance, the introduction of a new Social Fund, providing discretionary benefits and loans to low income families, may force local authorities to take a more active role in relation to the assessment of need (Walker and Walker, 1987, p. 37). In both the UK and the Netherlands, there have been central-local tensions, as a result of local government initiatives to offset national retrenchment policies.

Active Labour Market Policies

During the early part of the decade, considerable pessimism pervaded social security and employment policies. However, there are indications of a changing climate of opinion around the mid-1980s. One sign of this is the renewed effort to tackle unemployment with more comprehensive 'active' labour market measures. Whereas the most positive measures taken between the late 1970s and mid-1980s tended to be compensatory early retirement schemes, there is now a more substantial commitment to work creation and new job training schemes.

In Germany, for example, where active labour market programmes suffered severely from the earlier cuts, a new emphasis on work creation increased the numbers benefiting from Federal Labour Office schemes by 51 per cent between 1983 and 1985. In the UK, a wide range of employment initiatives for the young and long-term unemployed have been developed by the Department of Employment and the Manpower Services Commission (now known as the Training Agency). These include youth training programmes which offer a two-year place to virtually all 16 year-old school leavers. In Belgium, where there has been youth unemployment on a large scale, but also an increasing number of job vacancies, compulsory education was prolonged following 1983 and part-time schooling introduced, combining training and work (Vandenbroucke, 1987, pp. 54–5, 59–60).

These initiatives have not been confined to the northern countries. In Portugal, for example, recent years have seen a series of legislative measures and financial incentives to encourage the employment and self-employment of the unemployed, including the young unemployed in particular. In Greece, new schemes of vocational training, job placement, wage subsidy and job creation have been launched (Karantinos, 1987, p. 46ff.). Some give priority to disadvantaged groups (women, disabled, refugees and returning migrants) and disadvantaged areas.

It is worth noticing that many of these schemes are financed in part from the European Social Fund: something that is likely to become still more significant, with the expansion of the structural funds, as part of the progress towards the Single Market of 1992 (Commission of the European Communities, 1988b). On the other hand, changes in the ESF regulations has also brought some initiatives to an end. For example, in the mid-1980s, changes in the ESF regulations restricted training for the over-25s to those unemployed for more than a year. In consequence, some management training schemes run under Irish government auspices, using ESF money and targeted on the newly unemployed middle class, have had to be reduced (Wynne Jones, 1987).

Numerous other examples could be given of this growing commitment to work rather than welfare. However, none of these countries yet approaches the Swedish situation, where more than half the resources devoted to unemployment policy are spent on employment measures. Even in Denmark, where unemployment insurance is generous and the coverage broad by EC standards, the corresponding proportion is only about one fifth (Abrahamson et al., 1987, p. 12); and, indeed, following 1982 the new conservative-liberal government in Denmark cut back – and eventually abolished – the job creation programmes targetted on the young unemployed, which had been established by its social democratic predecessors, preferring to place its hopes in the capacity of the private sector to create jobs (ibid., p. 13).

In some countries, however, the increased commitment to work rather than welfare reflects fears that work incentives are being undermined by existing systems of income support. The Irish government has been among those concerned about the possible damage done to work incentives by social welfare benefits, especially in the case of the low paid. Here, as in the UK, the American notion of 'workfare' – relief to the unemployed only on condition of the performance of work tasks – has entered into policy debates during the mid-1980s (Kelleher, 1987, pp. 13–14; para. 4.3).

Finally, it is worth noticing that in some countries, there is a tradition of local authorities and/or public and charitable organisations 'employing' unemployed persons who are receiving unemployment allowance or social assistance, to carry out public works. In Belgium, since the 1930s public establishments and non-profit organisations with social, charitable or cultural objectives have had this possibility (Vandenbroucke, 1987, pp. 59–66): no contract exists between the person concerned and the organisation, but the labour exchange pays out an increased unemployment allowance, which varies according to the job which is held. This is, therefore, a rather different tradition from that in the UK, where proposals to demand work tests of the unemployed have, not least in recent times, encountered considerable hostility. But of course, in so far as such 'employment' does not involve the rights of industrial citizenship which the Commission of the European Communities is seeking to extend, as part of its Social Charter for European workers (see Chapter 1), it risks creating and perpetuating an industrial 'underclass', alongside the stratum of those who, as seen in the opening pages of this chapter, are neglected by the welfare system.

The Family and the Local Community

As seen in earlier chapters, the incidence of poverty among the elderly has fallen considerably in recent years, largely because of improvements in pensions arrangements. However, the growing numbers of the elderly – especially the very old – are imposing a growing burden on health and social services. Unless social protection expenditure keeps pace with these trends – and in many countries it is not doing so – the burden of care will, increasingly, fall on the family. However, during this same period there have been significant changes in family patterns (for example, increases in the rate of divorce and remarriage and in the female labour force participation rate) which have altered the composition of the household and have reduced the capacity of the family to care for its dependent members. Current public policy debates about welfare provision are, to some considerable extent, debates about the capacity and responsibility of the family to offer this care and support.

Recent years have seen a range of moves to reduce the traditional emphasis on institutional provision for the disabled, the elderly and other socially dependent groups. Attempts to develop 'community care' are now commonplace in the countries of the Community: independent living supported by community services, relatives, neighbours and friends. These moves have been prompted by attempts at cost-cutting by administrators and by criticism of the socially isolating effects of many institutions. However, the present period of austerity has meant that resources for developing community-based services for the dependent have been very limited; at the same time, the ability of families to care for their dependent members is weakened when unemployment reduces the resources of the younger members. These community care initiatives can only work where the people concerned are supported by a functioning network of social support; poorer people who lack such support will be left especially vulnerable, since they cannot themselves pay for alternatives. As seen earlier, these developments have implications for the 'feminisation' of poverty. Traditionally it was the women of the family who cared for the young and the old. In practice, 'community care' of the elderly and disabled often reinforces this role and means reliance on the unpaid labour of women.

As seen in earlier chapters, one of the most striking changes in family patterns has been the growth in the numbers of single parent families. Many of them depend on social assistance; and growing numbers of children are exposed to the risk of poverty. For most single parents, escape from the risk of poverty is most likely if they can be given 'access to employment opportunities and skills-training . . . : employment income is not only likely to be greater than that from an income support programme, it creates fewer barriers to transitions out of lone parenthood' (O'Higgins, 1987, p. 43). However, in a period of austerity, childcare facilities provided by government remain in general very limited, so that full-time employment and financial independence are difficult for single parents to achieve.

In some respects, these issues could be given still greater weight by the development of the Single Market. As already noted, the ability of families to care for their members, whether or not they are living together, is weakened when the standard of living of the younger members is reduced by unemployment; and at least in the short term, the Single Market is likely to bring increased unemployment to some regions and to some categories of the population. In addition, the programmes of structural transformation and economic development which the Commission expects to promote, particularly in the southern countries, may bring further disruptions to the traditional family structure: an alternative – and older – system of 'social security'. Those sections of the population who, as a result of rapid programmes of modernisation and urbanisation, lose this security are likely to find themselves particularly vulnerable to marginalisation and exclusion. These social costs of the Single Market could mean that the Commission will have to pay increasing attention to community development and family support, not just to economic development and training. These are, of course, areas of policy into which the Community institutions have as yet hardly ventured.

9.3 PUBLIC RESPONSIBILITY AND POLICY CHOICE

During the 1990s, social and demographic change, together with a heightened degree of economic insecurity, are likely to increase the demands on the social protection budgets of the countries of the European Community. During the immediate post-war period, this was not the case. In that period the main reason for the growth in social expenditures was the increasing level of benefits and increases in the unit cost of social services. However, during the coming years the ageing process will cause an endogenous rise of social expenditures for the elderly population, which will not be entirely offset by a decrease in social expenditure allocated to the younger population groups.

It is against this background that choices will need to be made as regards the protection that should be given to those population groups that are at particular risk of poverty and insecurity. Of course, these choices will be made in a variety of different contexts. For example, it may be valid in the more affluent European nations to relate new hardship among social minorities and widening social inequalities to populist anti-welfare state and anti-tax backlash; however, when one speaks of the 'dismantling of the welfare state' in Spain, for example, one must ask if it had ever existed at all. The same applies when one speaks of cutting 'social expenditures'.

In confronting these choices, public and official attitudes to the plight of the poor remain rather confused. In several countries, it seems that voters are becoming uneasy about poverty and are opposed to further social security cuts and retrenchment. In Denmark, for example, public sympathy for government measures to support those in need has increased since the mid-1970s (Hansen, 1986: see also Abrahamson, 1987, Appendix B). In Belgium, similarly, surveys carried out by the Ministry of Social Affairs indicate that among the population as a whole, the minimum social benefits which are deemed tolerable are considerably higher (at least 25 per cent) than the actual minimum benefits (DIMARSO, 1984; cf. Vandenbroucke, 1987, pp. 33–4). In the Netherlands, too, negative attitudes towards the unemployed appear to have diminished between the mid-1970s and the mid-1980s; and during the course of the 1980s, a larger proportion of Dutch society apparently came to believe that 'unemployed people should not be obliged to apply for jobs if there is no suitable job for them'. A similar decline is evident in the proportion of Dutch people who believe that social security abuse is widespread (Muffels and de Vries, 1987, pp. 16–18). There is a widespread view that social assistance benefits are too low (Sociaal en Cultural Planbureau, 1986).

Nevertheless, willingness to pay increased social security contributions is low. Rapid increases in social welfare benefits during the 1970s, coupled with economic slowdown and higher unemployment in the 1980s, both reducing the tax base for funding the benefits system, have produced an 'erosion of the community's will to fund the development of social services, including social security' (Irish Commission on Social Welfare, 1986, quoted in Kelleher, 1987, p. 17, para. 4.5). Moreover, there are a number of influential political actors who are promulgating views of poverty as an object of *self-help* and *charitable effort* rather than *political* action. The result – whether or not the intention – is to keep poverty – despite its extent – away from the centre of political debate. The *poor* are then seen as an object of charity and compassion (calling forth services of an 'assistantial' nature) or of admonitions to self-reliance (calling forth more punitive measures: workfare, etc.), rather than as inspiring political intervention aimed at securing changes in social and economic institutions. Both tendencies seem more likely to contribute to the persistence of poverty rather than to its elimination (da Costa, 1986, p. 2).

10 Inequality, Citizenship and Social Cohesion in the European Community

10.1 ON UNDERSTANDING THE NEW POVERTY

De Tocqueville, writing during the industrial transformations of the early nineteenth century, tried to understand the relationship between economic development and the generation of poverty in the Europe of his time. He pointed out that sudden changes in the international economy and in the demand for industrial products can, without warning, deprive large numbers of workers and their families of their means of livelihood. This vulnerability, which de Tocqueville cited as a principal cause of poverty in the first industrial revolution, has increased markedly during the equally dramatic transformations which are taking place in the industrial structures of today. The preceding pages have traced some of the resulting new patterns of poverty. The latter are not, however, confined to the advanced societies of the north. *Pace* de Tocqueville, it is evident that the patterns of poverty and inequality within the less advanced countries of southern Europe are closely dependent on the economic progress of their richer neighbours; and the completion of the internal market within the Community in 1992 will only emphasise this interrelationship.

De Tocqueville was interested less in the bare facts of income distribution than in the social and economic factors which destroy people's capacity to make ends meet and the institutional means which different societies have developed for supporting their dependent members. He feared that economic development would tend to multiply the numbers who must turn to public charity, something that he decried as being detrimental to work incentives; and he prescribed private charity as being a more suitable way of relieving need. If de Tocqueville were alive today, he would find some of his worst fears confirmed. In the northern countries increasing numbers of the population have used up their entitlement to insurance benefits and are resorting to social assistance. These benefits, the more they multiply, can greatly reduce the financial incentives to taking a job; and recipients can become imprisoned in a poverty trap of welfare dependency. Systems of social assistance are being made to bear a burden which is unprecedented during the post-war period; and in many countries this burden falls, in particular, on the local municipalities. In the face of this increasing pressure on public charity some governments are imposing more restrictive conditions on eligibility; but whether this resolves or merely transforms the problem is debatable. In the southern countries, where the family and the Church served traditionally as an alternative system of 'social security' and private charity, rapid programmes of modernisation and urbanisation mean that growing numbers of the population are losing the security of these traditional supports and find themselves particularly vulnerable to poverty.

The reference to de Tocqueville reminds us that it is *not* new for successive transformation of the economy to expose fresh groups of the population to the risk of poverty. However, as far as the post-war period is concerned, what *is* new about the 1980s is the widening range of the population which is subject to this economic insecurity. Added to this are insecurities which result from the transformation of the family: transformations, that is, in the system of *reproduction*; in particular, the growing numbers of single parent families and their vulnerability to poverty. Our social security systems seem to be incapable of coping with these two sources of increasing insecurity in the systems of production and reproduction; and we are forced again to confront de Tocqueville's question: how to provide support to a growing population of the poor.

These changes are not peculiar to our own continent. In the United States of America, elderly people form a declining proportion of the poor population, while unemployment and insecure employment are of increasing significance as causes of poverty. The number of single parent families in poverty has also been increasing: they grew from 25 per cent of the poor population in 1967 to more than 43 per cent in 1985 (Ruggles and Marton, 1986, p. 13). A majority of poor households which contain children are now headed by women (Sawhill, 1988). To some considerable extent, therefore, we are here discussing a problem of the First World, not just a problem of the European Community.

But perhaps these modern forms of poverty are not so serious after all. It is sometimes suggested that, at least in the northern countries, poverty today takes a rather mild and subjective form. After all, much of the conceptual debate in those countries has been concerned with *relative* poverty: goods and services which only a short time ago were defined as luxuries are now defined as necessities. It is therefore important to recognise that there is a harsher face to the poverty which has been developing in the 1980s. In many of our cities the number of homeless is increasing rapidly; and in countries such as the United Kingdom, considerable concern has been expressed at the dietary standards of the poor and unemployed and their children (Cole-Hamilton and Lang, 1986). It looks as though, in the north as well as in the south, these forms of 'absolute' poverty may be re-emerging to a more significant extent than at any time since the 1940s.

Of course, it can be argued that these problems of the 'new poverty' are only short term. For example, at least in the northern countries, the numbers of young people who are coming on to the labour market each year are falling rapidly, for normal demographic reasons. Other things being equal, we can expect this to exert a downward pressure on the unemployment statistics and to moderate the poverty statistics. There are, moreover, those who will argue that the impetus to economic expansion within the European Community which the common internal market of 1992 will provide will be enough to draw back into the labour market all but a hard core of the unemployed (Cecchini, 1988). Anti-poverty policies can then concentrate their attention on the non-able-bodied and those such as single parents, whose family responsibilities are such that they need continuing financial support from public funds. On this view, the new poor are the price that must be paid for the process of adjustment, but when this adjustment is complete, they will be reabsorbed into the new forms of production and prosperity.

However, it should be recognised that there is also a more pessimistic prognosis. Studies in France, for example, make it clear that many of the long-term unemployed are not particularly employable (poor qualifications, lack of occupational experience) (Stankiewicz, 1986); they are therefore far from being assured of a return to work, even if the labour market becomes tighter. More fundamentally, however, it seems clear that certain major changes are taking place in the economies of the First World: in particular, a growing bifurcation in the occupational structure, between highly skilled and well-paid jobs and the low skilled, low-paid and precarious. Those who lose their jobs may now be condemned to descend through a process of declassification into the unskilled sector at best, or very often into recurrent unemployment; and those who are seeking entry into the labour market for the first time may find it increasingly difficult to obtain secure employment.

Still worse, we may be creating a new 'underclass' within our still prosperous societies: a stratum of people whose energies lie unused, who represent a long-term burden on the public purse and who feel that they have no real stake in our societies. There are already areas in our cities with an unemployment rate of 70 per cent or more, where the majority of the residents, including the young people, can expect little, in present circumstances, except long-term dependence on welfare benefits. Many of these areas also include disproportionately high numbers of single parent families. Nor is this a development to which the most prosperous countries of the Community are immune. For example, a research group at Leyden University in the Netherlands points to 'the continuing deterioration of the lowest social security incomes . . . and the increasing charges on public services due to retrenchment policies of the government. A consequence of this may finally be that society becomes stratified into two major social groups in which the lowest stratum lives in unfavourable conditions, unemployment, few opportunities, poverty, bad housing conditions, etc.' (Hagenaars et al., 1987). Where there are additional divisions of ethnicity and race, the risks of exclusion are reinforced. The electoral successes of Le Pen in France show how readily ethnic hostilities can develop, when economic difficulties take away from the majority population its sense of security.

In the United States, the overwhelming predominance of black and Hispanic families among these inner city populations ensures that the underclass debate is, as much as anything, also a debate about race. Fears about the underclass are, however, only reinforced by the evident success of many middle-class blacks in moving outside the ghetto following the civil rights legislation of the 1960s, for the populations left behind are thereby dislocated and further deprived of their natural leaders. The spread of drugs and AIDS among these inner city communities, in such cities as New York, compounds the fears of social contamination; and the increasing resort to imprisonment as a means of social control seems to confirm to the wider public that these are criminal communities.

The American debates of the 1980s are clearly indebted to earlier controversies concerning poverty and marginalisation, such as those connected with Oscar Lewis' studies of the 'culture of poverty'

(Lewis, 1962) and the Moynihan Report on the disintegration of the Negro family (Moynihan, 1965; Rainwater and Yancey, 1967). However, some of the American scholars who are involved in the debates concerning the underclass have also begun to reassess the European experience and interpretation of marginalisation (Marmor et al., 1988). Their European counterparts, interested in the new patterns of poverty that have been emerging in the 1980s, will need to look back to those same earlier controversies, as well as to the current American debates, if they are to understand, first, the relationship between economic exclusion and the socio-cultural differentiation of marginalised groups; and, second, the social class identification and political role of such groups.

Thus, for example, in Germany, while most commentators during the 1960s and 1970s assumed that poverty was, at most, restricted to certain marginal groups of the population (*Randgruppen*), social researchers inspired by 'critical theory' took an increasing interest in such groups. The latter stood outside the mainstream of a society based on acquisitive individualism, which appeared to have distracted the main body of the working class from any effort to criticise and transform society. But increasingly, their analysis of these marginal groups came to focus attention upon the way that the latter were recruited from among the unemployed and the homeless, channelled to assistance agencies and metamorphosed in public consciousness into a separate and distinct type of sub-human being (Dennett et al., 1982, pp. 57–9, 173). The growing numbers of the homeless (*Nichtsesshaften*) in Germany today gives a revived relevance to these debates.

In France and the Benelux countries, the movement *Aide à Toute Détresse* (ATD) has managed to assimilate the recent concern about poverty and *precarité* to its long-standing interest in the marginalisation of the 'Fourth World'. It was in the 1950s, with reference to the population of the *bidonvilles*, that ATD first developed its message. This message, like the 'culture of poverty' theories of Oscar Lewis in the United States, emphasised both the social and economic marginality of this sub-proletariat and the distinctive sub-culture which gave them their positive identity. The public attention which has been given during the 1980s to emergency programmes of relief has allowed ATD to re-affirm the relevance of its analysis, even if the roots of the new poverty are, as seen in the preceding chapters of this book, distinctively different from those cited by ATD in the 1950s. As in the Catholic social welfare tradition to which ATD is in part indebted, the emphasis, however, is upon charitable and voluntary effort, mobilised by the ATD movement itself, as much as upon expanded social policies by the public authorities and political programmes of reform.

In Italy, social marginalisation was an equally important theme of scientific and political debate during the 1970s. This interest was born with the 'discovery' of the ghetto neighbourhoods ringing the big cities, with studies of the 'urban lumpen-proletariat', the poor peasants of the South, the world of illegal employment practices, marginality and deviance. A stringent debate developed concerning the class identification of these social strata and their economic, political and theoretical significance (Carbonard, 1979; Ferrarotti, 1974). Some commentators saw them as merely residual strata, awaiting integration into the mainstream of society. Others, however, viewed them as a new reality that demanded a radical re-working of existing accounts of class stratification; of the resulting interplay of social interests and alliances; and of the relationship between the political sphere and social movements. This discussion on marginality, moreover, was a long way from being purely scientific. The same years saw, for example, the development of community struggles centring on the relationship between marginalisation and the urban structure, on the structure of the housing market and social services, and on the relationship between illegal employment (or unemployment), marginalisation and deviance.

As in the recent American debates on the underclass, however, the Italian debates on marginalisation were also concerned with the social control mechanisms which, with the atrophy of the traditional fabric of the family and the local community, increasingly took the form of total institutions (Basaglia, 1975). The movement criticising the total institutions, taking psychiatry as its starting point, saw committal as a measure designed to control social strata which are excluded from the world of production and have become the object of specific definitions such as the mentally ill, the criminal, the invalid, etc. The total institutions were seen as the containment systems for those who have been excluded or are gradually being expelled from the world of production: containment which involves a further loss of personal rights, social relationships and cultural milieux. It is worth noticing that this movement developed in Italy during a period when institutionalisation began to affect visibly part of the middle classes.

These, then, are some of the longer-standing debates about marginalisation that will need to be incorporated into analyses of the 'new poverty', particularly if the tendencies towards a 'dual society' which were sketched earlier are reinforced. In the cities of southern Europe, illuminating comparisons may be available with the United States, where the very limited forms of welfare state provision leave the inhabitants of inner city communities unprotected and isolated as far as the wider society is concerned. But even in the northern countries, with their better established systems of social protection, political and scientific debate is beginning to consider the implications of a new stratum of long-term poor.

10.2 ON FIGHTING THE NEW POVERTY

The poverty which has been examined in the preceding chapters is a European – rather than a merely national – problem in at least two senses. First, it takes many similar forms in the different countries of the Community. Second, it is associated with wider social, economic and political changes which transcend national boundaries and which will be intensified by the creation of the Single Market in 1992. As the Commission of the European Communities has warned, the creation of the Single Market – at least in the short term – will bring significant social and economic dislocations, which will have 'very severe negative effects' for certain areas and certain categories of people. It warns, further, of 'social exclusion and marginalisation and the . . . appearance of new forms of poverty' (Commission of the European Communities, 1988b). The discussion in the preceding pages vindicates and gives substance to these fears.

Faced with this prospect, the Commission is concentrating its efforts on remedial measures through its structural funds, which support training and infrastructure investment in structurally backward regions and regions suffering industrial decline. These efforts must, however, be seen in the context of broader ranging efforts to promote active labour market policies by the governments of the Member States.

The Single European Act envisages an expanded role for the European Commission, in providing compensation for those population groups and regions which are placed at a disadvantage by the development of the Single Market and, more positively, in enabling them to take advantage of the opportunities which it offers. The recent legislation envisages, moreover, that the Commission will be much more actively engaged in negotiating European-funded programmes with local and regional government and with other partners active at that level, rather than going only through national authorities. In other words, the legislation acknowledges that the institutions of the European Community should be actively involved in the negotiation of working agreements and programmes of work which make use of European funding. To some extent, therefore, the European Community institutions, having set in motion the disruptive forces of the Single Market, are acknowledged as having a central responsibility for building a new 'settlement' between the various social actors concerned with the distribution of work and welfare in the countries of the Community.

At the same time, however, it is likely that the European authorities will have only limited scope for effective action in these fields. In the papers which the Commission has presented to the Council of Ministers, it emphasises the supposedly brief 'transition' period, during which adjustments to the new world of the Single Market will need to be assisted by special social measures. The Commission appears to take the view that the negative effects of the Single Market will be primarily short-term and can be fairly readily alleviated or compensated, until the long-term gains overwhelm them. This represents a political compromise by the Commission with liberal doctrines that the market will, except in abnormal times, tend towards equilibrium and towards the socially optimal utilisation of physical and human resources. As yet, little respect is paid to the view that the market system is inherently self-destabilising and liable to produce an economically and socially non-optimal use of resources (Goldthorpe, 1978).

It is difficult to predict what will be the result of the negotiations in which the European authorities are now to become engaged at local, regional and national level, in their efforts to combat – or to compensate for – the disadvantages imposed on certain population groups and regions by the development of the Single Market. What new alliances will develop between the actors at these different levels and how will they affect the orientation and functioning of social protection systems in particular? This is likely to depend crucially upon whether the European authorities themselves provide a clear lead; or whether, surrendering to the most powerful social actors in each country, they fail to press their own mandate in the task of social and political reconstruction.

The scope for effective European action in relation to the European problems of new poverty will depend, therefore, upon the sort of settlement that is worked out politically during the coming years between local, regional, national and European authorities. This political and constitutional settlement will help to shape the other 'settlements' which have figured in earlier chapters of this book: first, between the social classes; secondly, between the providers of welfare – public and private, religious and secular, local and national, professional and lay. However, one possible consequence of the closer integration which the Single Market will bring is that it may tend still further to undermine the truces which, in each of the countries concerned, have underpinned the welfare states of the post-war period. This is because closer integration may have the effect of breaking down the insulation between the social policy debates within different countries; and it may make it easier for critics of the *status quo* to draw unfavourable comparisons with policy and practice elsewhere and to develop political alliances on a cross-national basis. This improved communication may, in other words, mean that 'social inequities leap to universal attention . . . Conflicts long suppressed by separation and isolation escape the bounds that had confined them . . . as societies come into contact' (Schon, 1971, p. 26). In part, perhaps, because of this danger, the governments of the member states have left the social dimension of the internal market politically insecure and peripheral to the main policy-making processes of the European Community. The political weakness of the Commission means that it has little scope for giving the necessary leadership. However, without such leadership, what seems probable is that the political credibility of the European institutions themselves may be further undermined.

Nevertheless, more positive political futures are also possible. As noted in Chapter 1, the Commission of the European Communities, with the support of most member state governments, wants to guarantee to the citizen of the Community the right to dispose of his or her labour power untramelled by restrictions of nationality; to take part, through Community-wide systems of collective bargaining, in the decision-making processes by which the workplace is governed; and to enjoy certain basic minimum standards of health and safety in the working environment. These guarantees are all concerned with what can be broadly described as 'industrial citizenship' (Marshall, 1950) at a European level. Beyond this, the Commission is beginning to map out a still broader set of European social rights, not only for those in work but also for those who are outside the labour market (Commission of the European Communities, 1989).

This project need not produce the bleak uniformity feared by some member state governments. On the contrary, the Community may offer the opportunity, at a practical level, to exploit the diversity of the experience of its 12 member countries, in order to devise more effective responses to poverty and to other social issues. This exploitation is, indeed, already under way, in the small-scale programmes of cross-national action-research for which the Commission is already responsible in the anti-poverty and other related fields (Commission of the European Communities, 1988c). This sort of low-cost programme can, perhaps, promote the transfer of 'technologies' in the anti-poverty and other social fields and promote – at a practical level – the construction of the social dimension of the Single Market.

There is, of course, always the danger that this process of learning and technology transfer will be in one direction only: from the northern countries to those of the south. For reasons which can easily be understood, the southern countries are concerned to modernise their social systems and to adopt methods of intervention already developed in the north. However, it is important that in the anti-poverty field, as in other areas of social policy, the southern countries should define their own indigenous models of development, not least in order that they can offer new alternatives to the 'old' societies of the north. 'Harmonisation' within the Community need not preclude different paths of social welfare development by different countries, even if increasingly they draw upon and learn from each other's experience.

References

ABRAHAMSON, P., J. ANDERSEN, J. P. HENRIKSEN and J. E. LARSEN (1987) *Poverty and Poverty Politics in Denmark in the 1980s*, University of Copenhagen, Copenhagen.

BALSEN, W., H. NAKIELSKI, K. ROESSEL and R. WINKEL (1984) *Die Neue Armut*, Bund Verlag, Cologne.

BASAGLIA, F. (ed.) (1975) *Crimini di pace*, Einaudi, Turin.

BERGHMAN, J., H. DELEECK, E. de SMEET, P. JANSSENS, R. MARYNISSEN, L. SCHULPEN, E. SPEISSENS and R. van HOYE (1985) *Sociale Indicatoren van de Vlaamse Gemeeschap*, CBGS Monografie 1985/2, Ministry of the Flemish Community, Brussels.

BLUM-GIRADEAU, C. (1981) *Les Tableaux de la Solidarité*, Economica, Paris.

BOLZ, J (1987) *Poverty in the Federal Republic of Germany*, Working Paper No. 12, Centre for the Analysis of Social Policy, University of Bath.

BRANDOLINI, E. M. and V. RAZZANO (1987) *Poverty and Social Policies in Italy*, Istituto Ricerche Economiche e Sociali, Rome.

BRENTON, M. (1982) 'Changing Relationships in Dutch Social Services', *Journal of Social Policy*, vol. 11, pt 1, pp. 59–80.

CANTILLON, B., J. PEETERS and E. de RIDDER (1987) *Atlas van de sociale zekerheid in Belgie: kostprijs, financierung, sociale zekerheid*, Acco, Leuven-Amersfoort.

CARBONARD, A. (1979) *Povertà e classi sociali. Per la critica delle ideologie sui processi di pauperizzazione*, F. Angeli, Milan.

CARITAS ESPANOLA (1984) *Pobreza y Marginacion*, Documentation Social, Nos 56–7, Madrid.

CENTRAL BUREAU OF STATISTICS (1987) *Financial Report on Social Security*, 's-Gravenhage.

CERC (Centre d'Etudes des Revenus et des Couts) (1988) *Protection Sociale et Pauvreté*, La Documentation Francaise, Paris.

CECCHINI, P. (1988) *The European Challenge*, Wildwood House, Aldershot.

CHILD POVERTY ACTION GROUP (CPAG) (1986/7) *Poverty Magazine*, Winter, London.

CHILD POVERTY ACTION GROUP (CPAG) (1988) *Poverty: The Facts*, London.

CHURCH OF ENGLAND (1985) *Faith in the City*, Church House Publishing, London.

COLE-HAMILTON, I and T. LANG (1986) *Tightening Belts: A Report on the Impact of Poverty on Food*, The London Food Commission, London.

COMBAT POVERTY AGENCY (1988) *Poverty and the Social Welfare System in Ireland*, Dublin.

COMMISSION OF THE EUROPEAN COMMUNITIES (1981) *Final Report from the Commission to the Council on the First Programme of Pilot Schemes and Studies to Combat Poverty* (COM(81)769), December.

COMMISSION OF THE EUROPEAN COMMUNITIES (1987) *Third Periodic Report from the Commission on the Social and Economic Situation and Development of the Regions of the Community*, (COM(87)230), Brussels.

COMMISSION OF THE EUROPEAN COMMUNITIES (1988a) *Social Europe*, No. 3/88, Luxembourg.

COMMISSION OF THE EUROPEAN COMMUNITIES (1988b) *Social Dimension of the Internal Market*, (SEC(88)1148), Brussels.

COMMISSION OF THE EUROPEAN COMMUNITIES (1988c) *Interim Report on a Specific Community Action Programme to Combat Poverty* (COM(88)621 final), Brussels.

COMMISSION OF THE EUROPEAN COMMUNITIES (1988d) *European Economy* (Annual Economic Report, 1988–89), Brussels.

COMMISSION OF THE EUROPEAN COMMUNITIES (1989) *Community Charter of Fundamental Social Rights* (Preliminary Draft), (COM(89)248), Brussels, May.

COUNCIL OF THE EUROPEAN COMMUNITIES (1984) *Council Decision on Specific Community Action to Combat Poverty* (85/8/EEC).

da COSTA, A. B. (1986) 'Some Factors of Impoverishment in a Mediterranean Country: The Case of Portugal', paper prepared for the International Meeting of Experts on 'Poverty and Progress', UNESCO, Paris, November.

da COSTA, A. B. (1987) *Contextual Paper on Poverty in Portugal*, Working Paper No. 19, Centre for the Analysis of Social Policy, University of Bath.

da COSTA, A. B., M. SILVA, J. PEREIRINHA and M. MATOS (1985) *A Pobreza em Portugal*, Caritas, Lisbon.

DANMARKS STATISTIK (ed.) (1986) *Statistik Arbog*, Copenhagen.

de BARRA, O. (1984) 'Baling out the New Poor', *Sunday Press*, 30 September 1984, Dublin.

de BOECK, L. (1987) *Invloed van Regeringsmaatregelen op de koopkracht, 1981–86* (Influence of Governmental Measures on Purchasing Power, 1981–86), UIA Working Document, Antwerp.

de GREEF, M. H. G. and L. J. MIDDEL (1986) 'Problematische Schuldsituaties bij particulieren', in *Economische Statistische Berichten*, 19–11, pp. 1117–20.

DELEECK, H., L. de LATHOUWER and K. van den BOSCH (1988) *Social Indicators of Social Security*, Interim Report to the European Commission, University of Antwerp.

DENNET, J., E. JAMES, G. ROOM and P. WATSON (1982) *Europe Against Poverty: The European Poverty Programme 1975–1980*, Bedford Square Press, London.

DEPARTAMENTO CENTRAL DE PLANEAMENTO (1986) *Relatorio da Situacao Economica*, vol. 1, Lisbon.

DEPARTMENT OF EMPLOYMENT (1987) 'Ethnic Origin and Economic Status', *Employment Gazette*, January, pp. 18–29.

DEPARTMENT OF EMPLOYMENT (1989) 'Earnings and Hours of Manual Employees in October 1988', *Employment Gazette*, April, pp. 173–81.

DEPARTMENT OF HEALTH AND SOCIAL SECURITY (1986) *Low Income Families – 1983*, London.
DEPARTMENT OF HEALTH AND SOCIAL SECURITY (1988a) *Low Income Statistics: Report of a Technical Review*, London.
DEPARTMENT OF HEALTH AND SOCIAL SECURITY (1988b) *Low Income Families – 1985*, London.
DEPARTMENT OF HEALTH AND SOCIAL SECURITY (1988c) *Households Below Average Income: A Statistical Analysis: 1980–85*, London.
DEPARTMENT OF SOCIAL WELFARE (1987) *Statistical Information on Social Welfare Services*, Dublin.
de TOCQUEVILLE, A. (1835) *Memoir on Pauperism* (reprinted in English in *The Public Interest*, 1983, pp. 102–20).
DICKES, P., P. HAUSMAN and G. SCHABER (1980) *Niveau de Vie et Mode de Vie de Certains Ménages du Grand-Duché de Luxembourg*, CEPS, Luxembourg.
DIMARSO (1984) *Opinions of the Belgians regarding the Measures taken to Reform Social Security*, Brussels.
DIVOSA (1984) *Plaatsbepaling van DIVOSA*, 's-Gravenhage, Netherlands.
DONNISON, D. (1988) 'Defining and Measuring Poverty', *Journal of Social Policy*, vol. 17, pt 3, pp. 367–74.
DUPRÉ, J.-P., E. PASCHAUD and B. SIMONIN (1986) *Pauvreté-Précarité*, CREDOC, Paris.
DURAN, A. and P. LOPEZ-ARRIBAS (1987) *Poverty in Spain*, Working Paper No. 14, Centre for the Analysis of Social Policy, University of Bath.
ESPING-ANDERSEN, G. and W. KORPI (1984) 'Social Policy as Class Politics in Post-War Capitalism: Scandinavia, Austria and Germany', in J. H. Goldthorpe (ed.), *Order and Conflict in Contemporary Capitalism*, Clarendon Press, Oxford.
EUROSTAT (1988) *Population and Social Conditions*, Luxembourg.
FAMILY POLICY STUDIES CENTRE (1986) *Fact Sheet 3: One Parent Families*, London.
FERRAROTTI, F. (1974) *Vite da baraccati. Contributi ad una sociologia della marginalità*, F. Angeli, Milan.
FLORA, P. and J. ALBER (1981) 'Modernisation, Democratisation and the Development of Welfare States in Western Europe', in P. Flora and A. A. Heidenheimer (eds) (1981) *The Development of Welfare States in Europe and America*, Transaction Books, New Brunswick.
FLYNN, P. (1986) 'Urban Deprivation: What it is and how to Measure it', *Public Money*, vol. 6, no. 2.
GEISSLER, H. (1976) *Die Neue Soziale Frage*, Herder Verlag, Freiburg.
GEORGE, V. and R. LAWSON (eds) (1980) *Poverty and Inequality in Common Market Countries*, Routledge and Kegan Paul, London.
GIBBONS, L. (1984) 'Catherine the Great's Villages', in *The Poor Aren't News*, Simon Community, Dublin.
GOLDTHORPE, J. H. (1978) 'The Current Inflation: Towards a Sociological Account', in F. Hirsch and J. H. Goldthorpe (eds), *The Political Economy of Inflation*, Martin Robertson, London.
GOLDTHORPE, J. H. (1980) *Social Mobility and Class Structure in Modern Britain*, Clarendon Press, Oxford.

GOLDTHORPE, J. H. (1984) 'The End of Convergence: Corporatist and Dualist Tendencies in Modern Western Societies', in J. H. Goldthorpe (ed.), *Order and Conflict in Contemporary Capitalism*, Clarendon Press, Oxford.

GOLDTHORPE, J. H. (1985) 'Problems of Political Economy after the End of the Post-War Period', in C. S. Maier, (ed.), *Changing Boundaries of the Political*, Cambridge University Press, Cambridge.

HAGENAARS, A. J. M., K. de VOS and B. M. S. Van PRAAG (1987) *Arm en arm is twee*, 's-Gravenhage: Ministerie van Sociale Zaken en Werkgelegenheid.

HANSEN, E. J. (1986) *Danskernes levekar 1986 sammenholdt med 1976*, Hans Reitzels Forlag, Copenhagen.

HARRISON, P. (1983) *Inside the Inner City*, Penguin, Harmondsworth.

HARTMANN, H. (1985) 'Armut trotz Sozialhilfe', in S. Leibfried and F. Tennstedt (eds), *Politik der Armut und die Spaltung des Sozialstaats*, Suhrkamp Verlag, Frankfurt am Main.

HURSTFIELD, J. (1987) *Part-Timers: Under Pressure*, Low Pay Unit, London.

INSEE (Institut National de la Statistique et des Etudes Economiques (1987) *Données Sociales*, Paris.

IRISH COMMISSION ON SOCIAL WELFARE (1986) *Report of the Commission on Social Welfare*, The Stationery Office, Dublin.

ITALIAN COMMISSION ON POVERTY (1985) *La Povertà in Italia*, Presidenza Consiglio dei Ministri, Rome.

KAPTEYN, A., P. KOOREMAN, R. MUFFELS, et al. (1985) *Determinanten van bestaansonzekerheid; een vooronderzoek*, COSZ publication No. 10, Ministry of Social Affairs and Employment, 's-Gravenhage.

KARANTINOS, D. (1987) *Poverty and Anti-Poverty Policies in Greece*, Working Paper No. 13, Centre for the Analysis of Social Policy, University of Bath.

KELLEHER, P. (1987) *Poverty in Ireland: A National Contextual Paper*, Economic and Social Research Institute, Dublin.

KELLY, M. (1984) 'The Poor Aren't News', in *The Poor Aren't News*, Simon Community, Dublin.

KERR, C., J. T. DUNLOP, H. FREDERICK and C. A. MYERS (1964) *Industrialism and Industrial Man*, Oxford University Press, Oxford.

KING BAUDOUIN FOUNDATION (1987) *Armoede en Bestaansonzekerheid* (Poverty and Insecurity), 6 vols, Brussels.

KRAUS, F. (1981) 'The Historical Development of Income Inequality in Western Europe and the United States', in P. Flora and A. A. Heidenheimer (eds) (1981) *The Development of Welfare States in Europe and America*, Transaction Books, New Brunswick.

LAMMERTIJN, F. and D. LUYTEN (1987) *Rechthebbenden op het bestaansminimum*, Catholic University of Leuven.

LAWSON, R. (1979) *Social Assistance in the Member States of the European Community* (report prepared for the European Commission), University of Southampton.

LAWSON, R. (1986) 'Income Support during Unemployment: Comparisons

in Western Europe, 1945–85', in *European Institute of Social Security Yearbook 1985*, Kluwer, Deventer.
LENOIR, R. (1974) *Les Exclus: Un Francais sur Dix*, Seuil, Paris.
LEWIS, O. (1962) *Children of Sanchez*, Secker and Warburg, London.
LIPSET, S. M. (1964) 'The Changing Class Structure and Contemporary European Politics', *Daedalus*, Winter, pp. 271–303.
MACK, J. and S. LANSLEY (1985) *Poor Britain*, Allen and Unwin, London.
MARMOR, T. R., D. A. CHASSMAN and E. S. AULD (1988) *A Comparative Perspective on New Poverty and the Underclass* (report to the Rockefeller Foundation), Yale University.
MARSHALL, T. H. (1950) *Citizenship and Social Class*, Cambridge University Press, Cambridge.
MARTIN, J. and C. ROBERTS (1985) *Women and Employment: A Lifetime Perspective*, Department of Employment, London.
MEULDERS-KLEIN, M. T. and J. EEKELAAR (eds) (1988) *Family, State and Individual Economic Liberty*, 2 vols, Story-Scientia, Brussels.
MINISTÈRE DES AFFAIRES SOCIALES ET DE L'EMPLOI (1988) *Documents Statistiques*, No. 54 (May), Paris.
MORKEBERG, H. (1985) *Sociala Og Helbredsmaessige Konsekvenser as Arbejdsloshed*, Social Forsknings Instituttet, Copenhagen.
MOYNIHAN, D. (1965) *The Negro Family: The Case for National Action*, US Department of Labor, Washington DC.
MUFFELS, R. and A. de VRIES (1987) *Poverty in Debate: A Study of Evidence, Policy and Public Opinion on Poverty in the Netherlands*, University of Tilburg.
NATIONAL CENTRE FOR SOCIAL RESEARCH (EKKE) (1990) *Dimensions of Poverty in Greece*, Athens.
NELISSEN, J. and A. VOSSEN (1984) *Demografische ontwikkelingen en het sociaale zekerheidssysteem*, University of Tilburg, Tilburg.
NOLAN, B. (1987) *Relative Poverty Lines: An Application to Irish Data for 1973 and 1980*, Economic and Social Research Institute, Dublin.
NOLAN, B. (1989) *Measuring Poverty and the Impact of the Social Welfare System in Ireland*, Economic and Social Research Institute, Dublin.
NOLAN, B. and T. CALLAN (1989) 'Measuring Poverty over Time: Some Robust Results for Ireland 1980–87', *The Economic and Social Review*, vol. 20, no. 4, pp. 309–28.
OECD (Organisation for Economic Cooperation and Development) (1985) *New Policies for the Young*, Paris.
OECD (Organisation for Economic Cooperation and Development) (1988a) *The Future of Social Protection*, Paris.
OECD (Organisation for Economic Cooperation and Development) (1988b) *Employment Outlook*, Paris.
O'HIGGINS, M. (1987) *Lone Parent Familles in the European Community: Numbers and Socio-Economic Characteristics*, Working Paper No. 23, Centre for the Analysis of Social Policy, University of Bath.
O'HIGGINS, M. and S. JENKINS (1989) *Poverty in Europe: Estimates for the Numbers in Poverty in 1975, 1980, 1985*, paper presented to seminar on

Poverty Statistics held in Noordwijk, the Netherlands, in October, under the sponsorship of the Commission of the European Communities.
PIACHAUD, D. (1981) 'Peter Townsend and the Holy Grail', *New Society*, 10 September.
PIACHAUD, D. (1988) 'Poverty in Britain 1899 to 1983', *Journal of Social Policy*, vol. 17, pt 3, pp. 335–49.
PITROU, A. (1978) *La Vie Précaire: Des Familles face à leurs Difficultés*, CNAF, Paris.
RAINWATER, L. and W. L. YANCEY (1967) *The Moynihan Report and the Politics of Controversy*, Massachusetts Institute of Technology Press, Cambridge, Mass.
REES, T. (1988) *Poverty and the Young Unemployed in Europe*, University of Cardiff.
RICKETTS, E. and I. SAWHILL (1986) *Defining and Measuring the Underclass*, Urban Institute, Washington DC.
RINGEN, S. (1988) 'Direct and Indirect Measures of Poverty', *Journal of Social Policy*, vol. 17, pt 3, pp. 367–74.
ROCHE, J. (1984) *Poverty and Income Maintenance Policies in Ireland, 1973–80*, Institute of Public Administration, Dublin.
ROOM, G. (1982) 'The Cross-National Studies', in J. Dennett et al. (eds), *Europe Against Poverty*, Bedford Square Press, London.
ROOM, G., R. LAWSON and F. LACZKO (1989) '"New Poverty" in the European Community', *Policy and Politics*, vol. 17, no. 2, pp. 165–76.
RUGGLES, P. and W. P. MARTON (1986) *Measuring the Size of the Underclass: How Much do we Know?*, Urban Institute, Washington DC.
SARPELLON, G. (1983) *La Povertà in Italia*, Franco Angeli, Milan.
SAWHILL, I. (1986) *Anti-Poverty Strategies for the 1980s*, Urban Institute, Washington DC.
SAWHILL, I. (1988) 'Poverty in the US: Why is it so Persistent?', *Journal of Economic Literature*, vol. XXVI, pp. 1073–119.
SCHON, D. (1971) *Beyond the Stable State*, W. W. Norton, New York.
SEN, A. K. (1983) 'Poor Relatively Speaking', *Oxford Economic Papers*, vol. 35, pp. 153–69.
SOCIAAL EN CULTUREEL PLANBUREAU (1980) *Armoede in Nederland*, Rijswijk.
SOCIAAL EN CULTUREEL PLANBUREAU (1986) *Sociaal en cultureel rapport*, Rijswijk.
STANDING, G. (1986) *Unemployment and Labour Market Flexibility*, ILO, Geneva.
STANKIEWICZ, F. et al. (1986) *Revenu, Niveau de Vie et Devenir des Chômeurs de Longue Durée*, LAST-CLERSE, Lille.
STATISTISCHES BUNDESAMT (1970ff), *Sozialleistungen*, Stuttgart und Mainz.
STOLERU, L. (1974) *Vaincre la Pauvreté dans les Pays Riches*, Flammarion, Paris.
TOWNSEND, P. (1979) *Poverty in the United Kingdom*, Penguin, Harmondsworth.
VANDENBROUCKE, G. (1987) *Poverty in Belgium*, University of Antwerp.

VAN PRAAG, B. M. S., A. J. M. HAGENAARS and H. van WEEREN (1980) *Poverty in Europe*, COEPS, Leiden.

VEIT-WILSON, J. (1986) 'Paradigms of Poverty: A Rehabilitation of B. S. Rowntree', *Journal of Social Policy*, vol. 15, pt 1, pp. 69–99.

VEIT-WILSON, J. (1987) 'Consensual Approaches to Poverty Lines and Social Security', *Journal of Social Policy*, vol. 16, pt 2, pp. 183–211.

WALKER, R., R. LAWSON and P. TOWNSEND (eds) (1984) *Responses to Poverty: Lessons from Europe*, Heinemann, London.

WALKER, C. and A. WALKER (1987) *Poverty in Great Britain*, University of Sheffield.

WILSON, W. J. (1985) 'The Urban Underclass in Advanced Industrial Society', in P. E. Peterson (ed.), *The New Urban Reality*, Brookings Institute, Washington DC.

WRESINSKI, J. (1987) *Grande Pauvreté et Précarité Economique et Sociale*, Avis et Rapports du Conseil Economique et Social, Paris.

WYNNE JONES, G. (1987) 'Whatever Happens to Redundant Managers?', *Management*, vol. 34, no. 5, pp. 16–19 (Dublin).

Index